Berlitz®

Dani

phrase book & dicti

HAVFRUEN

Berlitz Publishing
New York London Singapore

Contacting the Editors
Every effort has been made to provide accurate information in this publication, but changes are inevitable. The publisher cannot be responsible for any resulting loss, inconvenience or injury. We would appreciate it if readers would call our attention to any errors or outdated information. We also welcome your suggestions; if you come across a relevant expression not in our phrase book, please contact us at: **comments@berlitzpublishing.com**

Twelfth Printing: May 2018
Printed in China

Editor: Helen Fanthorpe
Translation: updated by Wordbank
Cover Design: Rebeka Davies
Interior Design: Beverley Speight
Picture Researcher: Tom Smyth

Cover Photos: all images iStock and Shutterstock
Interior Photos: APA/David Hall 1, 15, 25, 39, 48, 56, 64, 80, 101, 104, 110, 134, 139, APA Rudy Hemmingsen 14, 98, 99 106, 109, Istockphoto 36, 52, 136, 142, 144, 149, 155, Lucy Johnston 166, Mina Patria 42, Beverley Speight 50.

Distribution

UK, Ireland and Europe
Apa Publications (UK) Ltd
sales@insightguides.com
United States and Canada
Ingram Publisher Services
ips@ingramcontent.com
Australia and New Zealand
Woodslane
info@woodslane.com.au
Southeast Asia
Apa Publications (SN) Pte
singaporeoffice@insightguides.com

Worldwide
Apa Publications (UK) Ltd
sales@insightguides.com

Special Sales, Content Licensing, and CoPublishing
Discounts available for bulk quantities. We can create special editions, personalized jackets, and corporate imprints. sales@insightguides.com; www.insightguides.biz

Contents

Food & Drink

People

Leisure Time

Special Requirements

In an Emergency

Dictionary

Pronunciation

This section is designed to make you familiar with the sounds of Danish by using our simplified phonetic transcription. You'll find the pronunciation of the Danish letters and sounds explained below, together with their 'imitated' equivalents. This system is used throughout the phrase book: simply read the pronunciation as if it were English, noting any special rules below.

Stress has been indicated in the phonetic transcription with underlining. Bold on vowels indicates a lengthening of the vowel sound.

Consonants

Letter	Approximate Pronunciation	Symbol	Example	Pronunciation
c	1. before e, i, y, like s in sit	s	**citron**	see·_troan_
	2. before a, o, u and K a consonant, like k in kite	k	**cafeteria**	kah·feh·_teh_·ree·a
d	1. at the end of the word after a vowel, or between a vowel and unstressed e or i, like th in this1	dh	**med**	medh
	2. otherwise, as in English	d	**dale**	_da_·ler

1 The letter **d** is not pronounced in **nd** and **ld** at the end of a word or syllable (**guld** = gooll), or before unstressed **e**, **t** or **s** in the same syllable (**plads** = plass).

Letter	Approximate Pronunciation	Symbol	Example	Pronunciation
g	1. at the beginning of a word or syllable, like g in go	**g**	**glas**	_glas_
	2. otherwise, like y in yet[2]	**y**	**sige**	_see•yer_
hv	like v in view	**v**	**hvor**	_voar_
j, hj	like y in yet	**y**	**ja**	_ya_
k	1. between vowels, like g in go	**g**	**ikke**	_ig•ger_
	2. otherwise like k in kite	**k**	**kaffe**	_kah•fer_
ng	like ng in sing	**ng**	**ingen**	_ing•ern_
p	1. between vowels, like b in bit	**b**	**stoppe**	_stoh•ber_
	2. otherwise like p in pill	**p**	**pude**	_poo•dher_
r	at the beginning of a word, pronounced in the back of the throat, but otherwise often omitted	**r**	**rose**	_roa•ser_
s	like s in see	**s**	**skål**	_skowl_

[2] The letter **g** occasionally sounds like **ch** in Scottish loch and can sometimes be mute after **a**, **e**, **o**.

Letter	Approximate Pronunciation	Symbol	Example	Pronunciation
sj	usually like sh in sheet	**sh**	**sjælden**	_sheh•lern_
t	1. between vowels, like d in do	**d**	**lytte**	_lew•der_
	2. otherwise like t in to[3]	**t**	**torsk**	_toarsk_

Letters b, f, h, l, m, n, v are generally pronounced as in English.

Vowels

Letter	Approximate Pronunciation	Symbol	Example	Pronunciation
a	1. when long, like a in father	**ah**	**klare**	_klah•rah_
	2. when short, like a in cat	**a**	**hat**	_hat_
e	1. when long, like er in fern	**er**	**svare**	_svah•rer_
	2. when short, like e in met	**eh**	**let**	_leht_
i	1. when long, like ee in bee	**ee**	**ile**	_ee•ler_
	2. when short, like i in pin	**i**	**drikke**	_drig•ger_

[3] In nouns that end with an **e**, an **r** is added to create the plural. In verbs that end with an **e**, an **r** at the end indicates the first person form. This **er** sound, in both cases, sounds like **ah**.

Letter	Approximate Pronunciation	Symbol	Example	Pronunciation
o	1. when long, like oa in boat	**oa**	**sol**	_soal_
	2. when short, like o in lot	**oh**	**godt**	_goht_
u	1. when long, oo in pool	**oo**	**frue**	_froo•er_
	2. when short, like oa in boat	**oa**	**luft**	_loaft_
y	like ew in new	**ew**	**nyde**	_new•dher_
æ	1. when long, like ay in day	**ay**	**sæbe**	_say•ber_
	2. when short, like e in get	**eh**	**ægte**	_ehg•ter_
ø	like ur in fur	**ur**	**frøken**	_frur•kern_
å	1. when long, like ow in tow	**ow**	**åben**	_ow•bern_
	2. when short, like aw in saw	**aw**	**sådan**	_saw•dan_

A vowel is generally long in stressed syllables when it's the final letter or followed by only one consonant. If followed by two or more consonants, or in unstressed syllables, the vowel is generally short. In or after some vowels, a short puff of air (glottal stop) is added following the sound. The glottal stop significantly changes the meaning of certain words, e.g., **tænder** with a glottal stop means 'teeth', whereas **tænder** without a glottal stop means 'to turn on'. As foreigners will be understood without using the glottal stop, this sound has not been included in the phonetics.

Sound Combinations

Letter	Approximate Pronunciation	Symbol	Example	Pronunciation
av, af	like	**ow**	**hav**	*how*
ej, eg	like ie in lie	**ie**	**nej**	*nie*
ev	like e in get plus oo sound	**eu**	**levned**	*leu•nerdh*
ov	like ow in show	**ow**	**sjov**	*show*
øj	ike oi in oil	**oi**	**øje**	*oi•er*
øv	like o in so	**oh**	**søvnig**	*soh•nee*

Dansk (Danish), a North Germanic language related to Norwegian, Swedish and Icelandic, is the official language of Denmark.

There are about six million native speakers in Denmark and parts of northern Germany.

Danish is an official language of the autonomous territories of Greenland and the Faroe Islands, in addition to Greenlandic and Faroese.

How to use this Book

Sometimes you see two alternatives separated by a slash. Choose the one that's right for your situation.

ESSENTIAL

I'm here on vacation [holiday]/business. **Jeg er her på ferie/forretningsrejse.** *yie ehr hehr paw fehr•yer/foh•reht•nings•rie•ser*

I'm going to... **Jeg skal til...** *yie skal til...*

I'm staying at the... Hotel. **Jeg bor på Hotel...** *yie boar paw hoa•tehl...*

Words you may see are shown in YOU MAY SEE boxes.

YOU MAY SEE...

TOLD	customs
TOLDFRIE VARER	duty-free goods
VARER AT ANGIVE	goods to declare

Any of the words or phrases listed can be plugged into the sentence below.

At the Hotel

Does the hotel have...? **Har hotellet...?** *hah hoa•tehl•erdh...*

a computer **en pc** *ehn peh•seh*

an elevator [a lift] **en elevator** *ehn eh•ler•va•toh*

(wireless) internet **(trådløst) internet** *(trowdh•lurst) in•tah•neht*

room service **service på værelset** *sur•vees paw vehrl•serdh*

Danish phrases appear in purple.

Read the simplified pronunciation as if it were English. For more on pronunciation, see page 7.

Relationships

I'm...	**Jeg er...** *yie ehr...*
married	**gift** *geefd*
divorced	**skilt** *skild*
I'm widowed.	**Jeg er enkemand *m* /enke *f*.** *yie ehr ehn•ker•man/ehn•ker*

For Numbers, see page 159.

Related phrases can be found by going to the page number indicated.

When different gender forms apply, the masculine form is followed by *m*; feminine by *f*

In Denmark, upon meeting, it is customary to shake hands for both men and women. Close friends (male-female/female- female) may give kisses on the cheeks. As a greeting, you could say **Går det godt?** (How's it going?) or **Hva så?** (What's up?). **Hej** (general greeting) in Danish is used both for hello or hi and bye.

Information boxes contain relevant country, culture and language tips.

Expressions you may hear are shown in You May Hear boxes.

YOU MAY HEAR...

Næste! *nehs•der*

Din billet/Dit pas, tak. *deen bee•lehd/deet pas tahk*

Next!

Your ticket/passport, please.

Color-coded side bars identify each section of the book.

Survival

Money

ESSENTIAL

Where's...?	**Hvor er...?** *voar ehr...*
the ATM	**pengeautomaten** *pehng·er·ow·toa·ma·dern*
the bank	**banken** *bahnk·ern*
the currency exchange office	**vekselkontor** *vehk·serl·kohn·toar*
What time does the bank open/close?	**Hvornår åbner/lukker banken?** *voar·naw owb·nah/loa·gah bahnk·ern*
...to change ...ounds into	**Jeg vil gerne veksle nogle dollars/pund til kroner.** *yie vil gehr·ner vehks·ler noa·ler doh·lahs/poon til kroa·ner*
	Jeg vil gerne indløse en rejsecheck. *yie vil gehr·ner in·lur·ser ehn rie·ser·shehk*

...fer
...are
...many
...ay
...sdays.
...exchange
...

...veksle penge her? ko...
...hr

...lkursen? k...

...e·ner kawd

...wd veer·gah ig·ger

...kort.
...h meet kawd

...nt kort. *yie vil kawd*

Arrival & Departure

ESSENTIAL

I'm here on vacation [holiday]/business.	**Jeger her på ferie/forretningsrejse.** *yie ehr hehr paw fehr·yer/foh·reht·nings·rie·ser*
I'm going to...	**Jeg skal til...** *yie skal til...*
I'm staying at the ...Hotel.	**Jeg bor på Hotel...** *yie boar paw hoa·tehl...*

YOU MAY HEAR...

Din billet/Dit pas, tak. *deen bee·lehd/deet pas tahk*
Your ticket/passport, please.

Hvad er formålet med din rejse? *vadh ehr foh·mow·lehdh medh deen rie·ser*
What's the purpose of your visit?

Hvor skal du bo? *voar skal doo boa*
Where are you staying?

Hvor lang tid skal du være her? *voar langh teedh skal doo vay·er hehr*
How long are you staying?

Hvem rejser du sammen med? *vehm rie·ser doo sahm·ern medh*
Who are you with?

Border Control

I'm just passing through.	**Jeg er her kun på gennemrejse.** *hehr koon paw geh·nehm·rie·ser*
I would like to declare...	**Jeg vil gerne fortolde...** *yie vil gehr for·toh·ler...*
I have nothing to declare.	**Jeg har ikke noget at fort...** *yie har ig·ger noa·erdh ad foh...*

YOU MAY SEE…

INDSÆT DIT KORT	insert card
ANNULLER	cancel
SLET	clear
INDTAST	enter
PINKODE	PIN
UDBETALING	withdraw funds
FRA DIN CHECKKONTO	from checking [current] account
FRA DIN OPSPARINGSKONTO	from savings account
KVITTERING	receipt

Cash can be obtained from **pengeautomater** (ATMs), which are located throughout Denmark. Some debit cards (with the Plusand Cirrus logos) and most major credit cards are accepted. Be sure you know your PIN and whether it is compatible with European machines, which usually expect a four-digit, numeric code. ATMs o good rates, though there may be some hidden fees.

Vekselkontor (currency exchange offices) and **banker** (banks) options for exchanging currency. Exchange offices are found in tourist centers. Banks in Copenhagen are open Monday to Frid 9:30 a.m. to 4:00 p.m., with some branches open late on Thu Currency exchange offices and banks charge similar fees to money. Remember to bring your passport for identificatio

My credit cards were stolen.	**Mine kort er blevet stjålet.** _m_ ehr _bleh_•verdh _stjow_•lerd
My card doesn't work.	**Mit kort virker ikke.** _meed k_
The ATM ate my card.	**Pengeautomaten tog mit** _Pehng_•er•ow•toa•ma•dern t

For Numbers, see page 159.

YOU MAY HEAR…

Har du noget at fortolde? har doo noa•erdh
_ad for•_tohl_•ler_

Du skal betale told af det her. doo skal
_beh•_ta•_ler tohl a deh hehr_

Vær venlig at åbne denne taske. vehr vehn•lee Pleas
_ad_ owb_•ner_ deh_•ner_ tas_•ger_

Do you have
anything to
You must
on this,
ba

YOU MAY SEE…

TOLD
TOLDFRIE VARER
VARER AT ANGIVE
VARER AT ANGIVE

YOU MAY SEE...

Denmark, Norway and Sweden all use the same name for their currency, but the value differs in each country. The **krone** (meaning 'crown', pronounced _kroa•ner_ and abbreviated **kr.** or **DKK**), is divided into 100 øre (pronounced _ur•er_).
Coins: 25 and 50 **øre**, 1, 2, 5, 10 and 20 **kroner**
Notes: 50, 100, 200, 500 and 1,000 **kroner**

Getting Around

ESSENTIAL

How do I get to town?	**Hvordan kommer jeg ind til byen?** _voar•_dan_ kohm•ah yie in til _bew•_ern
Where's...?	**Hvor er...?** _voar ehr..._
the airport	**lufthavnen** _loaft•hown•ern_
the train [railway] station	**togstationen** _tow•sta•shoa•nern_
the bus station	**busstationen** _boos•sta•shoa•nern_
the subway [underground] station	**metrostationen** _meh•troa•sta•shoan•nern_
How far is it?	**Hvor langt er der?** _voar lahngt ehr dehr_
Where can I buy tickets?	**Hvor køber man billetter?** _voar _kur•_ber man bee•_leh•_dah_
A one-way/ return ticket.	**En enkeltbillet/returbillet.** _ehn ehn•kerld•bee•lehd/reh•_toor_•bee•lehd_
How much?	**Hvor meget koster det*?** _voar _mie•_erdh _kohs•_dah deh_
Are there any discounts?	**Er der nogen rabatter?** _ehr der noa•ern rah•_ba•_dah_
Which...?	**Hvilken...?** _vil•_kern..._

gate	**gate** *gayd*	
line	**tog** *tow*	
platform	**perron** *peh·rohng*	
Where can I get a taxi?	**Hvor kan jeg få en taxa?** *voar kan yie fow ehn tahk·sa*	
Take me to this address.	**Kør mig til denne adresse.** *kur mie til deh·ner a·drah·ser*	
Where can I rent a car?	**Hvor kan jeg leje en bil?** *voar kan yie lie·er ehn beel*	
Can I have a map?	**Har du et vejkort?** *har doo eht vie·kawd*	

For Grammar, see page 156.

Tickets

When's...to Århus?	**Hvornår afgår...til Århus?** *voar·naw ow·gaw...til aw·hoos*
the first bus	**den første bus** *dehn fur·sder boos*
the next flight	**det næste fly** *deh nehs·der flew*
the last train	**det sidste tog** *deh sees·der tow*
Where can I buy tickets?	**Hvor køber man billetter?** *voar kur·berman bee·lehd·ah*
One ticket/Two tickets, please.	**En billet/To billetter, tak.** *ehn bee·lehd/toa bee·leh·dah tahk*
For today/tomorrow.	**Til i dag/i morgen.** *til ee·dah/ee·mawn*
A (an)...ticket.	**...billet.** *...bee·lehd*
one-way [single]	**En enkelt** *ehn ehn·kerld*
return trip	**En retur** *ehn reh·toor*
first class	**En førsteklasse** *ehn furs·der kla·ser*
business class	**En business class** *ehn beesh·nesh klass*
economy class	**En økonomiklasse** *ehn ur·koa·noa·mee·kla·ser*

How much?	**Hvor meget?**	*voar mie·erdh*
Is there a discount for...?	**Er der rabat for...?**	*ehr dehr rah·bat foh...*
children	**børn**	*burn*
students	**studerende**	*stoo·deh·reh·ner*
senior citizens	**pensionister**	*pang·shoa·nees·dah*
tourists	**turister**	*tuh·rist·ehr*
The express bus/ express train, please.	**Hvor er ekspresbussen/lyntoget?** *voar ehr ehks·prehs boo·sern/lewn· tow·erdh*	
The local bus/train, please.	**Hvor er lokalbussen/regionaltoget?** *voar ehr loa·kal·boo·sern/reh·gee·onal· tow·erdh*	
I have an e-ticket.	**Jeg har en e-billet.** *yie har ehn eh·bee·lehd*	
Can I buy a ticket on the bus/train?	**Kan jeg købe en billet i bussen/toget?** *kan yie kur·ber ehn bee·lehd ee boo·sern/tow·erdh*	
Do I have to stamp the ticket before boarding?	**Skal jeg stemple billetten, inden jeg står på?** *skal yie stem·pler bee·lehden, in·ern yie staw pow*	
How long is this ticket valid?	**Hvor længe gælder billetten?** *voar layng·er gayl·dehr bee·lehd·ern*	
Can I return on the same ticket?	**Kan jeg komme tilbage med samme billet?** *kan yie kohm·ah til·ba·yer medh sahm·ern bee·lehd*	
I'd like to...my reservation.	**Jeg vil gerne...min bestilling.** *yie vil gehr·ner...meen beh·stil·ing*	
cancel	**annullere**	*a·noo·leh·rah*
change	**ændre**	*ehn·drer*
confirm	**bekræfte**	*beh·krehf·der*

For Days, see page 161.

For Time, see page 161

Plane

Airport Transfer

How much is a taxi to the airport?	**Hvor meget koster en taxa til lufthavnen?** _voar mie·erdh kohs·dah ehn tahk·sa til loaft·how·nern_
I would like to go to...Airport, please.	**Jeg vil gerne til... Lufthavn, tak.** _yie vil gehr·ner til...loaft·hown tahk_
My airline is...	**Jeg skal flyve med...** _yieskalflew·er medh..._
My flight leaves at...	**Mit fly afgår klokken...** _meet flew ow·gaw kloh·gehrn..._
I'm in a rush.	**Jeg har travlt.** _yie har trowlt_
Can you take an alternate route?	**Kan du køre ad en anden rute?** _kan doo kur·rah adh ehn a·nern roo·ter_
Can you drive faster/slower?	**Kan du køre hurtigere/langsommere?** _kan doo kur·er hoor·dee·ah/lang·sohm·ah_
For Time, see page 161.	

Checking In

Where is the check-in desk for flight...?	**Hvor er check-in skranken for fly...?** _voar ehr chek·in skrahng·gern foh flew..._
My name is...	**Mit navn er...** _meet nown ehr..._
I'm going to...	**Jeg skal til...** _yie skal til..._

YOU MAY SEE...

ANKOMST	arrivals
AFGANG	departures
AFGANGSGATES	departure gates
CHECK-IN SKRANKE	check-in desk
E-BILLET CHECK-IN	e-ticket check-in
BAGAGEBÅND	baggage claim
INDENRIGSFLY	domestic flights
UDENRIGSFLY	international flights

I have...	**Jeg har...**	*yie hah*
one suitcase	**en kuffert**	*ehn koa•fahd*
two suitcases	**to kufferter**	*toh koa•fahd•ehr*
one piece of hand luggage	**Et styk håndbagage**	*eht stewk hawn•ba•ga•sher*
How much luggage is allowed?	**Hvor meget baggage må jeg have med?**	*voar mie•erdh ba•ga•sher mow yie ha medh*
Is that pounds or kilos?	**Er det pund eller kilo?**	*ehr deh poon eh•ler kee•loa*
Which gate does flight... leave from?	**Hvilken gate afgår fly...fra?**	*vil•gern gayd ow•gaw flew...frah*
I'd like a window/an aisle seat.	**Jeg vil gerne bede om et vinduessæde/sæde ved midtergangen.**	*yie vil gehr•ner beh ohm ehd vin•doos•say•dher/say•dher vedh mi•dah•gahng•ern*
When do we leave/arrive?	**Hvornår flyver/ankommer vi?**	*voar•naw flew•ah/an•kohm•ah vee*
Is there any delay on the flight...?	**Er fly... forsinket?**	*ehr flew... foh•sing kerdh*
How late will it be?	**Hvor forsinket er det?**	*voar foh•sing•kerdh ehr deh*

Luggage

Where is/are...?	**Hvor er...?** *voar eher...*
the luggage trolleys	**bagagevognene** *ba•ga•sher•vow•nehr•ner*
the luggage lockers	**bagageboksene** *ba•ga•sher•bohk•ser•ner*
the baggage claim	**bagagebåndene** *ba•ga•sher•bawn•er•ner*
My luggage has been lost.	**Min bagage er gået tabt.** *meen ba•ga•sher erh gow•erdh tahbt*
My luggage has been stolen.	**Min bagage er blevet stjålet.** *meen ba•ga•sher erh bleh•verdh stjow•lerdh*

YOU MAY HEAR...

Næste! *nehs•der*	Next!
Din billet/Dit pas, tak. *deen bee•lehd/deet pas tahk*	Your ticket/passport, please.
Hvor mange stykker baggage har du? *voar mahng•er sdur•ger ba•ga•sher hah doo*	How many pieces of luggage do you have?
Du har for meget baggage med. *doo hah foh mie•erdh ba•ga•sher mehdh*	You have excess baggage.
Den er for tung/stor som håndbagage. *dehn ehr foh toang/stoar som hawn•ba•ga•sher*	That's too heavy/ large for a carry-on [to carry on board].
Har du selv pakket dine tasker? *hah doo sehl pah•kehrd dee•ner tas•ger*	Did you pack these bags yourself?
Har nogen bedt dig om at tage noget med? *hah noa•ern behd die ohm ad ta noa erdh mehdh*	Did anyone give you anything to carry?
Tøm dine lommer. *turm dee•ner loh•mah*	Empty your pockets.
Tag dine sko af. *ta dee•ner skoa a*	Take off your shoes.
Nu begynder vi at boarde fly... *noo beh•gur•nah vee ad boar•der flew...*	Now boarding flight...

| My suitcase was damaged. | **Min kuffert er blevet beskadiget.** *meen koa•fahd erh bleh•verdh beh•ska•dhee•erd* |

Finding your Way

Where is…?	**Hvor er…?** *voar eher…*
the currency exchange office	**vekselkontoret** *vehk•serl•kohn•toar•erd*
the car hire	**biludlejningen** *beel•oodh•lie•ning•ern*
the exit	**udgangen** *oodh•gahng•ern*
the taxi rank	**taxaholdupladsen** *tahk•sa•hohl•er•pla•sern*
the metro [underground]	**metroen** *meh•troa•ern*
Is there a bus/train into town?	**Kører der en bus/et tog ind til byen?** *kur•rah dehr ehn boos/eht tow in til bew•ern*

For Asking Directions, see page 34

Train

How do I get to the train station?	**Hvordan kommer jeg hen til togstationen?** *voar•dan kom•er yie hehn til tow•sta•shoa•nern*
Is it far?	**Er det langt herfra?** *ehr deh lahngd hehr•frah*
Where is/are…?	**Hvor er…?** *voar ehr…*

The Danish train network connects towns across the main islands and the Jutland peninsula. Which train you choose depends on your destination and how quickly you want to get there. **S-bane** or **S-tog** is a commuter train, which serves Copenhagen and surrounding areas. Regional trains and **InterCity** (express) trains travel between Copenhagen and other parts of the country. The **Øresund** train connects Copenhagen and Malmö, Sweden.

A number of discounts are offered depending on the traveler (students, senior citizens, groups, families and children receive considerable reductions), day and time of travel (off-peak times are more highly discounted) as well as the destination. S-trains, the metro and buses run on an integrated network, so you may transfer without paying any additional cost. Keep in mind that buying a **rabatkort** (10-trip ticket), valid for a specified number of zones, is cheaper than buying single tickets. You may also want to consider a 24- hour or 72-hour **CPHCARD** (Copenhagen Card), which offers unlimited train, bus and metro transportation, free entry to over 60 museums and attractions and other discounts. The **CPHCARD** can be purchased online, at tourist offices, in the airport and at major train stations.

the ticket office	**billetlugen**	bee·*lehd*·loo·ern
the information desk	**informationslugen**	in·foh·ma·*shoans*·loo·ern
the luggage lockers	**bagageboksene**	ba·*ga*·sher·bohk·ser·ner
the platforms	**perronerne**	pehr·*rohng*·ah·ner
I'd like a schedule [timetable].	**Jeg vil gerne bede om en køreplan.**	yie vil *gehr*·ner beh ohm ehn *kur*·ah·plan
How long is the trip [journey]?	**Hvor længe tager turen?**	voar *layng*·er tah *too*·rern
Is it a direct train?	**Er det et direkte tog?**	ehr deh ehd dee·reik·ter tow

Do I have to change trains?	**Skal jeg skifte tog?** *skal yie skeef·der tow*
Is the train on time?	**Kommer toget til tiden?** *koh·mer tow·erdh til teedh·ehn*

For Asking Directions, see page 34

For Tickets, see page 20.

Departures

Which platform does the train to...leave from?	**Fra hvilket spor afgår toget til...?** *frah vil·kerdh spoar ow·gaw tow·erdh til...*
Is this the track [platform] to...?	**Er det her den rigtige perron til...?** *ehr deh hehr dehn rig·tee·er pehr·rohng til...*
Where is track [platform]...?	**Hvor er perron nummer...?** *voar ehr pehr·rohng noa·mah...*
Where do I change for...?	**Hvor skal jeg skifte tog til...?** *voar ska yie skeef·der tow til...*

On Board

Can I sit here/open the window?	**Kan jeg sidde her/åbne vinduet?** *kan yie si·dher hehr/ owb·ner vin·doo·eht*
Is this seat taken?	**Er denne siddeplads optaget?** *ehr dehn·er si·dher·plas op·ta·erdh*
I think that's my seat.	**Det er vist min siddeplads.** *deh ehr vist meen si·dher·plas*
Here's my reservation	**Her er min reservation** *hehr ehr meen reh·sah·va·shoan*

YOU MAY SEE...

TIL PERRONERNE	to the platforms
INFORMATION	information
PLADSRESERVERINGEN	reservations
ANKOMST	arrivals
AFGANG	departures

Bus

Where's the bus station?	**Hvor ligger busstationen?** *voar li•gah boos•sta•shoa•nern*
How far is it?	**Hvor langt er der?** *voar langt ehr dehr*
How do I get to…?	**Hvordan kommer jeg til…?** *voar•dan koh•mah yie til…*
Does the bus stop at…?	**Stopper bussen ved…?** *stoh•bah boo•sern vedh…*
Can you tell me when to get off?	**Vil du sige til, når jeg skal af?** *vil doo see•yer til naw yie skal a*
Do I have to change buses?	**Er det nødvendigt at skifte bus?** *ehr deh nurdh•vehn•deed ad skeef•der boos*
Stop here, please!	**Jeg skal af her!** *yie skal a hehr*

For Tickets, see page 20.

Danish buses often continue travel where train lines end. Combining bus and train travel is very easy. You'll find that many bus stations are located next to train stations, their arrival and departure schedules are closely timed and you can use your train ticket to continue your trip on the bus or vice versa. Taking the bus or combining train and bus travel is in fact often faster than train-only travel since many bus connections are more direct than train connections.

YOU MAY SEE…

BUSSTOP	bus stop
INDGANG/UDGANG	enter/exit
DU SKAL STEMPLE DIN BILLET	stamp your ticket

YOU MAY HEAR...

Alle i toget! _a_·ler ee _tow_·erdh

Billetter, tak. bee·_lehd_·ah tahk

Du skal skifte i... doo skal _skeef_·der ee...

Næste stop er... _neehs_·der stohp ehr...

All aboard!

Tickets, please.

You have to change at...

Next stop...

Metro

Where's the nearest metro (subway) station?	**Hvor er den nærmeste metrostation?** voar ehr dehn _nehr_·meh·ster _meh_·troa·sta·shoan
Which line for...?	**Hvilket tog skal jeg tage til...?** _vil_·kerdh tow skal yie ta til...
Which direction?	**Hvilken retning?** vil·kern reht·ning
Where do I change for...?	**Hvor skal jeg skifte til...?** voar skal yie _skeef_·der til...
Is this the right train for...?	**Kører det her tog til...?** _kur_·rah deh hehr tow til...
How many stops to...?	**Hvor mange stationer er der til...?** voar mahng·er sta·shoa·nehr ehr dehr til
Where are we?	**Hvor er vi henne?** voar ehr vee _heh_·ner

For Tickets, see page 20

Copenhagen's **Metro** (subway) is a clean, quick and convenient way to travel through the city. You can purchase a **rabatkort** (10-trip ticket) or a 24-hour or 72-hour **CPHCARD** (Copenhagen Card) for discounted fares. Tickets for the **Metro** are interchangeable with those for buses and trains. Tickets must be stamped on the platform before boarding. Note that traveling without a valid ticket may lead to a sizeable fine.

Denmark is comprised of some 500 islands. Though most of the larger islands are linked by bridges, ferries are a way of life in Denmark. There is regular local as well as international ferry service from Denmark to the Baltic States, England, Germany, Norway, Poland and Sweden. Passenger and car reservations can be made in advance via any travel agency.

Boat & Ferry

When is the next boat to…?	**Hvornår går den n æste båd til…?**	voar·_naw_ gaw dehn _nes_·der bowdh til…
Can I take my car?	**Må jeg tage min bil med?**	mow yie ta meen beel medh
What time is the next sailing?	**Hvornår afholdes den næste sejlads?**	voar·naw ow·hohl·es dehn neehs·der siy·lahs
Can I book a seat/ cabin?	**Kan jeg booke et sæde/kahyt?**	Kan yie book·er eht say·dher/ka·hewt
How long is the crossing?	**Hvor længe tager overfarten?**	voar layng·er tah ow·ah·fah·dehn

For Tickets, see page 20.

YOU MAY SEE…

REDNINGSBÅD	life boats
REDNINGSVEST	life jackets

Taxi

Where can I get a taxi?	**Hvor kan jeg få en taxa?**	voar kan yie fow ehn _tahk_·sa

YOU MAY HEAR...

Hvor skal du hen? *voar skal doo hehn* — Where to?

Hvad er adressen? *vadh ehr a·drah·sern* — What's the address?

Can you send a taxi?	**Kan du sende en taxi?** *kan doo seh·ner ehn tahk·sa*
Do you have the number for a taxi?	**Har du nummeret på en taxi?** *har doo noa·mahrdh paw ehn tahk·sa*
I'd like a taxi now/for tomorrow at...	**Jeg vil gerne bestille en taxa nu/til i morgen klokken...** *yie vil gehr·ner beh·sti·ler ehn tahk·sa noo/til ee moh·wern kloh·gehrn ...*
Pick me up at (place/time)...	**Hent mig på/klokken...** *hehnt mie paw/kloh·gehrn...*
Please take me to...	**Kør mig til...** *kur mie til...*
this address	**denne adresse** *deh·ner a·drah·ser*
the airport	**lufthavnen** *loaft·how·nern*
the train station	**togstationen** *tow·sta·shoa·nern*
I'm in a hurry.	**Jeg har travlt.** *yie hah trowlt*
Can you drive faster/slower?	**Kan du køre hurtigere/langsommere?** *kan doo kur·ah hoor·dee·ah/lang·sohm·ah*
Stop/Wait here.	**Stands/Vent her.** *stans/vehnd hehr*
How much?	**Hvor meget koster det?** *voar mie·erdh kohs·dah deh*

Taxis can be hailed in the street. Just look for the **FRI** (free) sign. Taxis can also be found at taxi stands at airports and train stations or ordered by phone. All cabs are metered and service charges are included in the fare, so tipping is not necessary. Most taxis accept credit cards; however, if you're not carrying cash, be sure to check first.

| You said…kroner. | **Du sagde…kroner.** *doo sa•er…kroa•nah* |
| Keep the change. | **Behold byttepengene.** *beh•hohl bew•der•pehng•ah•ner* |

Bicycle & Motorbike

I'd like to hire…	**Jeg vil gerne leje…** *yie vil gehr•ner lie•er…*
a bicycle	**en cykel** *ehn sew•gerl*
a moped	**en knallert** *ehn kna•lahd*
a motorcycle	**en motorcykel** *ehn moa•tah•sew•gerl*
How much per day/ week?	**Hvad koster det per dag/uge?** *Vadh kohs•dah deh pehr da/oo•er*
Can I have a helmet/ lock?	**Kan jeg få en hjelm/lås?** *kan yie fow ehn yehlm/lows*

Cycling is very much a part of daily life in Denmark and a regular means of transportation for many Danes. Great investment has been made in recent years to keep Copenhagen bike-friendly, prompting it to be labeled the 'City of Cyclists' of late. Bikes may be borrowed, free of charge, at one of the approximately 125 City Bike Parking spots around the city. All you have to do is leave a deposit that is returned to you when you bring the bike back to any City Bike Parking rack.

Car Hire

Where can I hire a car?	**Hvor kan jeg leje en bil?** *voar kan yie lie•er ehn beel*
I'd like to hire…	**Jeg vil gerne leje…** *yie vil gehr•ner lie•er…*
a cheap/small car	**en billig/lille bil** *ehn bee•lee/lee•ler beel*
a 2-door/4-door car	**en to-dørs/fire-dørs bil** *ehn toa•durs/ feer•durs beel*

an automatic	**en bil med automatgear** *ehn beel mehdh ow·toa·mad geer*
a manual car	**almindeligt gear** *al·meen·deh·leet geer*
a car with air-conditioning	**en bil med klimaanlæg** *ehn beel medh klee·ma·an·layg*
a car seat	**et barnesæde** *eht bah·ner·say·dher*
How much is it…?	**Hvor meget koster det…?** *voar mie·erdh kohs·dah deh…*
per day/week	**per dag/uge** *pehr da/oo·er*
per kilometer	**per kilometer** *pehr kee·loa·meh·dah*
for unlimited mileage	**med ubegrænset kørsel** *medh oo·beh·grehn·serdh kur·sehl*
with insurance	**med forsikring** *medh foh·sik·ring*
Are there any discounts for…?	**Er der nogen specialtilbud…?** *ehr dehr noa·ern speh·shal·til·boodh…*

YOU MAY HEAR…

Har du et internationalt kørekort?
har doo et in·tah·na·shoa·nalt kur·rah·kawd
Do you have an international driver's license?

Må jeg se dit pas? *mow yie seh deet pas*
May I see your passport?

Ønsker du at tegne forsikring? *urn·sgah doo ad tie·ner for·sik·ring*
Do you want insurance?

Du skal betale et depositum på… *doo skal beh·ta·ler eht deh·poa·see·toam paw…*
There's a deposit of…

Underskriv venligst her. *oa·nah·sgreev vehn·leesd hehr*
Sign here.

Fuel Station

Where's the nearest fuel station?	**Hvor er den nærmeste benzinstation?** *voar ehr dehn <u>nehr</u>•mer•ster behn•<u>seen</u>•sta•shoan*
Fill it up, please.	**Fuld tank, tak.** *fool tahnk tahk*
... liters, please.	**...liter benzin.** *...<u>lee</u>•dah behn•<u>seen</u>*
I'd like to pay in cash/ by credit card.	**Jeg vil gerne betale kontant/med kreditkort.** *yie vil <u>gehr</u>•ner beh•<u>ta</u>•ler kohn•<u>tant</u>/mehdh kreh•<u>deet</u>•kawd*

YOU MAY SEE...

95 OKTAN	regular
98 OKTAN	super
DIESEL	diesel

Asking Directions

Are we on the right road for...?	**Er det den rette vej til...?** *ehr deh dehn <u>reh</u>•der vie til...*
How far is it to...?	**Hvor langt er der til...?** *voar lahngt ehr dehr til...*
Where's...?	**Hvor er...?** *voar ehr...*
...Street	**...gade** *...<u>ga</u>•dher*
this address	**denne adresse** *<u>deh</u>•ner ah•<u>drah</u>•ser*
the highway [motorway]	**motorvejen** *<u>moa</u>•tah•vie•ern*
Can you show me on the map?	**Kan du vise mig det på kortet?** *kan doo <u>vee</u>•ser mie deh paw <u>kaw</u>•derdh*
I'm lost.	**Jeg er faret vild.** *yie ehr <u>fah</u>•erdh veel*

Parking

Is there a parking lot [car park] nearby?	**Er der en parkeringsplads i nærheden?** *Ehr dehr ehn pah•<u>keh</u>•rings•plas ee <u>nehr</u>•heh•dhern*
Can I park here?	**Må jeg parkere her?** *Mow yie pah•<u>keh</u>•ah hehr*

YOU MAY HEAR...

igeud _lee·er·oodh_	straight ahead
til venstre _til vehn·sdrah_	on the left
til højre _til hoi·ah_	on the right
på/rundt om hjørnet _paw/roundt ohm yur·nerdh_	on/around the corner
overfor... _ow·ah·foh..._	opposite...
bagved... _ba·vehdh..._	behind...
ved siden af... _vehdh see·dhern a..._	next to...
efter... _ehf·dah..._	after...
nord/syd _noar/sewdh_	north/south
øst/vest _ursd/vehsd_	east/west
ved trafiklyset _vedh trah·feeg·lew·serdh_	at the traffic light
ved vejkrydset _vehdh vie·krew·serdh_	at the intersection

Where's the parking garage/parking meter?	**Hvor er parkeringsgaragen/ parkometeret?** _Voar ehr pah·keh·rings·gah·rah·ghehn pah·ko·meh·dah·reht_
How much is it...?	**Hvor meget koster det...?** _voar mie·erdh kohs·dah deh..._
per hour	**per time** _pehr tee·mer_

Parking in Denmark is restricted. Metered zones allow up to three hours of parking. In Copenhagen, in unmetered zones, there are ticket vending machines where you can pay with coins and bills or by credit card. The ticket should be in a visible place on the dashboard of your car.

| per day | **per dag** *pehr da* |
| overnight | **for natten** *foh <u>na</u>•dern* |

Breakdown & Repair

My car broke down/ won't start.	**Min bil har fået motorstop/vil ikke starte.** *Meen beel har <u>fow</u>•erdh <u>moa</u>•tah•stohb/ vil <u>ig</u>•ger <u>stah</u>•der*
Can you fix it (today)?	**Kan du reparere den (i dag)?** *kan doo reh•pah•<u>rehr</u> dehn (ee•dah)*
When will it be ready?	**Hvornår er den klar?** *voar•<u>naw</u> ehr dehnklah*
How much?	**Hvor meget koster det?** *voar <u>mie</u>•erdh <u>kohs</u>•dah deh*
I have a puncture/ flat tyre (tire)	**Jeg har et punkteret/fladt dæk** *yie har ehd punh•te•rehd/fladht deck*

Accidents

| There's been an accident. | **Der er sket en ulykke.** *dehr ehr skeht ehn <u>oo</u>•lew•ger* |
| Call an ambulance/ the police. | **Ring hurtigt efter en ambulance/ politiet.** *ring <u>hoor</u>•deet ehf•dah ehn ahm•boo•<u>lahng</u>•ser/poa•lee•tee•erdh* |

Places to Stay

ESSENTIAL

Can you recommend a hotel?	**Kan du anbefale et hotel?**	kan doo _an_•beh•fa•ler eht hoa•_tehl_
I have a reservation. My name is...	**Jeg har bestilt værelse.** yie har beh•_stild_ _vehrl_•ser **Mit navn er...** meet nown ehr...
Do you have a room...?	**Har I et værelse...?** har ee ehd _vehrl_•ser...	
for one/two	**enkeltværelse/dobbeltværelse** _ehn_•kerld•vehrl•ser/_doh_•berld•vehrl•ser	
with a bathroom	**med bad** mehdh badh	
with air conditioning	**med klimaanlæg** mehdh _klee_•ma•an•layg	
for tonight	**for i nat** for ee nad	
for two nights	**for to nætter** for toa _nay_•dah	
for one week	**for en uge** for ehn _oo_•er	
How much?	**Hvor meget koster det?** voar _mie_•erdh _kohs_•dah deh	
Do you have anything cheaper?	**Har du noget billigere?** har doo _noa_•erdh _bee_•leer	
When's check-out?	**Hvornår skal vi tjekke ud?** voar•_naw_ skal vee _tjeh_•ker oodh	
Can I leave this in the safe?	**Må jeg lade dette være i boksen?** mow yie la _deh_•ter _vay_•er i _bohk_•sern	
Can I leave my bags?	**Må jeg lade mine tasker være her?** mow yie la mee•ner _tas_•gah _vay_•ah hehr	
Can I have the bill/ a receipt?	**Kan jeg få regningen/en kvittering?** kan yie fow _rie_•ning•ern/ehn kvee•_teh_•ring	
I'll pay in cash/by credit card.	**Jeg vil gerne betale kontant/med kreditkort.** yie vil _gehr_•ner beh•_ta_•ler kohn•_tahnt_/mehdh kreh•_deet_•kawd	

Somewhere to Stay

Can you recommend…?	**Kan du anbefale et hotel?** *kan doo*
a hotel	<u>an</u>•beh•fa•ler eht hoa•<u>tehl</u>
a hostel	**et hostel** *ehd hos•tehl*
a campsite	**en campingplads** *ehn kahm•ping•plas*
a bed and breakfast	**et bed and breakfast** *ehd bed and breakfast*
What is it near?	**Hvad ligger det i nærheden af?** *vadh li•gah*
	deh ee <u>nehr</u>•heh•dhern a
How do I get there?	**Hvordan kommer jeg derhen?** *voar•<u>dan</u>*
	<u>koh</u>•mer yie dehr•<u>hehn</u>

At the Hotel

I have a reservation.	**Jeg har en reservation.** *yie hah ehn*
	reh•sah•va•<u>shoan</u>
My name is…	**Mit navn er…** *meet nown ehr…*
Do you have	**Har I et ledigt værelse…?** *hah ee edh*
a room…?	<u>leh</u>•dheed vehrl•ser…
with a toilet/	**med toilet/brusebad**
shower	*medh toa•ee•lehd/ broo•ser•badh*
with a bathroom	**med bad** *mehdh badh*
with air	**med klimaanlæg** *mehdh <u>klee</u>•ma•an•layg*
conditioning	
that's smoking/	**ryger/ikke-ryger** <u>rew</u>•ah/ig•ger <u>rew</u>•ah
non-smoking	
for tonight	**for i nat** *foh ee nad*
for two nights	**for to nætter** *foh toa <u>nay</u>•dah*
for one week	**for en uge** *foh ehn <u>oo</u>•er*
Does the hotel have…?	**Har hotellet…?** *hah hoa•<u>tehl</u>•erdh…*
a computer	**en pc** *ehn peh <u>seh</u>*
an elevator [a lift]	**en elevator** *ehn eh•ler•<u>va</u>•toh*
(wireless) internet	**(trådløst)internet** *(<u>trowdh</u>•lurst) <u>in</u>•tah•neht*

In Denmark, there is a variety of places to stay in addition to hotels, which range from one to five stars. You could choose to stay in a bed and breakfast, such as a **kro** (country inn), in an old **slot** (castle) or a **motel** (motel). If you are traveling by car, good options include vandrerhjem (a hostel), **ungdomsherberg** (a student hotel) or **sommerhus** (a summer house), which refers to any rented living space, such as a seaside cottage or apartment. For a unique vacation experience, you might choose a **bondegårdsferie** (farmhouse stay), which lets you taste Danish farm life firsthand.

Advanced reservations are recommended particularly during the high season. If you arrive in Denmark without a reservation, tourist information offices can assist in locating places to stay as can the Room Reservation Service, found at Central Train Station in Copenhagen.

room service	**service på værelset** <u>sur</u>•vees paw <u>vehrl</u>•serdh
a gym	**et motions center** ehd moa•<u>shoan</u>•sehn•dah
I need…	**Jeg skal bruge…** yie skal broo•er…
an extra bed	**en ekstra seng** ehn <u>ehk</u>•strah sehng
a cot	**en klapseng** ehn <u>klahp</u>•sehng
a crib	**en barneseng** ehn <u>bah</u>•ner•sehng

YOU MAY HEAR...

Må jeg bede om dit pas/kreditkort.
mow yie beh ohm deet pas/kreh·deet·kawd

Your passport/credit card, please.

Udfyld venligst denne formular. *oodh·fewl vehn·leesd deh·ner foh·moo·lah*

Fill out this form.

Underskriv venligst her. *oa·nah·sgreew vehn·leesd hehr*

Sign here.

Price

How much per night/ week?	**Hvad koster det per nat/uge?** *vadh kohs·dah deh pehr nad/oo·er*
Does the price include breakfast/sales tax [VAT]?	**Inkluderer prisen morgenmad/moms?** *in·kloo·deh·ah pree·sern mawn·madh/mawms*
Are there any discounts?	**Kan jeg få rabat?** *kan yie fow rah·badh*

Preferences

Can I see the room?	**Må jeg se værelset?** *mow yie seh vehrl·serdh*
I'd like a...room.	**Jeg vil gerne have et ... værelse.** *yie vil gehr·ner ha ehd... vehrl·ser.*
better	**bedre** *bedh·rah*
bigger	**større** *stur·rah*
cheaper	**billigere** *bee·leer*
quieter	**mere roligt** *meh·rah roh·lidt*
I'll take it.	**Jeg tager det.** *yie tah deh*
No, I won't take it.	**Nej, jeg vil ikke have det.** *nie, yie vil ig·ger ha deh*

Questions

| Where's...? | **Hvor er...?** *voar ehr...* |
| the bar | **baren** *bah·ern* |

YOU MAY SEE...

SKUB/TRÆK	push/pull
TOILET	restroom [toilet]
BRUSER	shower
ELEVATOREN	elevator [lift]
TRAPPE	stairs
VASKERI	laundry
VIL IKKE FORSTYRRES	do not disturb
BRANDDØR	fire door
NØDUDGANG	emergency exit
MORGENVÆKNING	wake-up call

Where's...?	**Hvor er...?**	*voar ehr...*
the restroom [toilet]	**toilettet**	*toa·ee·leh·derdh*
the elevator [lift]	**elevatoren**	*eh·ler·va·tohn*
Can I have...?	**Kan jeg få...?**	*kan yie fow...*
a blanket	**et tæppe**	*eht teh·ber*
an iron	**et strygejern**	*eht strew·er·yehrn*
the room key/	**nøglen/kortet til værelset**	
key card		*noi·lern/kaw·derdh til vehrl·serdh*
a pillow	**en pude**	*ehn poo·dher*
soap	**noget sæbe**	*noa·erdh say·ber*
toilet paper	**noget toiletpapir**	*noa·erdh toa·ee·led·pah·peer*
a towel	**et håndklæde**	*eht hawn·klay·dher*
Do you have an adapter for this?	**Har I en adapter til denne her?**	*har ee ehn a·dahp·tah til deh·ner hehr*
How do I turn on the lights?	**Hvordan tænder jeglyset?**	*voar·dan tay·ner yie lew·serdh*
Can you wake me at...?	**Kan du vække mig klokken...?**	*kan doo vay·ger mie klohg·gehrn...*

Can I have my things from the safe?	**Må jeg få mine ting i boksen?** *mow yie fow <u>mee</u>•ner ting ee <u>bohk</u>•sern*
Is there any mail/a message for me?	**Er der noget post/nogen beskeder til mig?** *ehr dehr <u>noa</u>•erdh pohst/<u>noa</u>•ern beh•<u>sgeh</u>•dhah til mie*
Do you have a laundry service?	**Har I vasketøjsservice?** *hah ee vas•ger•turys•sur•vees*

Problems

There's a problem.	**Der er et problem.** *dehr ehr eht proa•<u>blehm</u>*
I've lost my key/key card.	**Jeg har tabt min nøgle/mit nøglekort.** *yie hah tahbd meen <u>noi</u>•ler/meet <u>noi</u>•ler•kawd*
I've locked myself out of my room.	**Jeg har låst mig ude af mit værelse.** *yie hah lowsd mie <u>oo</u>•dher a meet <u>vehrl</u>•ser*
There's no hot water/ toilet paper.	**Der er ikke noget varmt vand/ toiletpapir.** *dehr ehr <u>ig</u>•ger <u>noa</u>•erdh vahmd van/toa•ee•<u>lehd</u>•pah•peer*
The room is dirty.	**Værelset er beskidt.** *<u>vehrl</u>•serdh ehr beh•<u>skeed</u>*
There are bugs in our room.	**Der er insekter på værelset.** *dehr ehr in•<u>sehg</u>•tah paw <u>vehrl</u>•serd*
…doesn't work.	**…er i uorden.** *…ehr ee <u>oo</u>•oh•dern*

Can you fix…?	**Kan du reparere…?** *kan doo reh·pah·<u>reh</u>·ah…*
the air-conditioning	**klimaanlægget** <u>klee</u>·ma·an·layg
the fan	**ventilatoren** *vehn·tee·la·shoan*
the heat [heating]	**varmen** *<u>vah</u>·mern*
the light	**lyset** *<u>lew</u>·serdh*
the TV	**fjernsynet** *<u>fyehrn</u>·sew·nerdh*
the toilet	**toilettet** *toa·ee·<u>leh</u>·derdh*
Can I get another room?	**Kan jeg få et andet værelse?** *can yie fow eht <u>an</u>·erdh <u>vehrl</u>·ser*

> Danish electricity is generally 220 volts, though many camping sites also have 110-volt plugs available. British and American appliances will need an adapter.

Checking Out

When do I have to check out?	**Hvornår skal jeg tjekke ud?** *voar·<u>naw</u> skal yie <u>tyay</u>·ger oodh*
Can I leave my bags here until…?	**Må jeg lade mine tasker stå her indtil…?** *mow yie la <u>mee</u>·ner <u>tas</u>·gah stow hehr <u>in</u>·til…*
Can I have an itemized bill/a receipt?	**Må jeg bede om en udspecificeret regning/kvittering?** *mow yie beh ohm ehn oodh·speh·see·fee·seh·redh <u>rie</u>·ning/ kvee·<u>teh</u>·ring*
I think there's a mistake in this bill.	**Jeg tror, der er en fejl i regningen.** *yie troar dehr ehr ehn fiel ee <u>rie</u>·ning·ern*
I'll pay in cash/by credit card.	**Jeg vil gerne betale kontant/med kreditkort.** *yie vil <u>gehr</u>·ner beh·<u>ta</u>·ler kohn·<u>tant</u>/mehdh kreh·<u>deet</u>·kawd*

In Denmark, **moms** (sales tax or value-added tax) and service charges are included in your bill in hotels and restaurants, in admissions charges and purchase prices as well as taxi fares. Tips may be given for outstanding service, but they are not necessary.

Renting

I've reserved an apartment/a room.	**Jeg har reserveret en lejlighed/et værelse.** *yie hah reh·sah·veh·rerdh ehn lie·lee·hehdh/eht vehrl·ser*
My name is...	**Mit navn er...** *meet nown ehr...*
Can I have the key/key card?	**Må jeg bede om nøglen/nøglekortet?** *mow yie beh ohm noi·lern/noi·ler·kaw·derdh*
Are there...?	**Findes der...?** *fin·ners dehr...*
dishes	**spisestel** *spee·ser·stehl*
pillows	**puder** *poo·dhah*
sheets	**lagener** *la·ner*
towels	**håndklæder** *hawn·klay·dhah*
kitchen utensils	**køkkenredskaber** *kur·ken·redh·skab·ah*
When/Where do I put out the bins/recycling?	**Hvornår/Hvor skal jeg sætte skraldet ud/genbrug?** *voar·naw/voar skal yie seh·der skrah·lerdh oodh/gehn·broo oodh*
... is broken.	**...er i uorden.** *...ehr ee oo·oh·dern*
How does...work?	**Hvordan fungerer...?** *voar·dan fung·geh·rah...*
the air conditioner	**klimaanlægget** *klee·ma·an·lay·gerdh*
the dishwasher	**opvaskemaskinen** *ohb·va·sker·ma·skee·nern*
the freezer	**fryseren** *frew·sern*
the heater	**varmen** *vah·mern*
the microwave	**mikroovnen** *mee·kroa·ow·nern*

the refrigerator	**køleskabet** <u>kur</u>·ler·ska·berdh
the stove	**ovnen** <u>ow</u>·nern
the washing machine	**vaskemaskinen** <u>vas</u>·ger·ma·skee·nern

Domestic Items

I need...	**Jeg skal bruge...** _yie skal <u>broo</u>·er..._
an adapter	**en adapter** _ehn a·dahb·dah_
aluminum foil	**aluminiumsfolie** _a·loo·<u>mee</u>·nee·oums·foal·yer_
a bottle opener	**en oplukker** _ehn <u>ohb</u>·loa·ger_
a broom	**en kost** _ehn kowsd_
I need...	**Jeg skal bruge...** _yie skal <u>broo</u>·er..._
a can opener	**en dåseåbner** _ehn <u>dow</u>·ser·<u>owb</u>·nah_
cleaning supplies	**rengøringsartikler** _<u>rehn</u>·gur·rings·ah·teek·lah_
a corkscrew	**en proptrækker** _ehn <u>prohb</u>·tray·gah_
detergent	**vaskemiddel** _vas·ker·<u>mee</u>·dherl_
dishwashing liquid	**opvaskemiddel** _<u>ohb</u>·vas·ker·mee·dherl_
bin bags	**skraldeposer** _<u>skrah</u>·ler·poa·sah_
a light bulb	**en pære** _ehn <u>pay</u>·ah_
matches	**tændstikker** _<u>tehn</u>·sti·kah_
a mop	**en moppe** _ehn <u>moh</u>·ber_
napkins	**papirservietter** _pah·<u>peer</u>·sehr·vee·<u>eh</u>·dah_
paper towels	**papirhåndklæder** _pah·<u>peer</u>·hawn·klay·dhah_
plastic wrap [cling film]	**plastfolie** _<u>plast</u>·foal·yer_
a plunger	**en svupper** _ehn swob·ah_
scissors	**en saks** _ehn saks_
a vacuum cleaner	**en støvsuger** _ehn <u>sturw</u>·soo·ah_

For In the Kitchen, see page 76

For Oven Temperatures, see page 165.

At the Hostel

Do you have any places left for tonight?	**Har I nogen ledige pladser i nat?** *hah ee noa·ern leh·dhi·yer plas·sah ee nad*
Can I have…?	**Kan jeg få…?** *kan yie fow…*
a single/double room	**et enkeltværelse/dobbeltværelse** *eht ehn·kerld·vehrl·ser/doh·berld·vehrl·ser*
a blanket	**et tæppe** *eht tay·ber*
a pillow	**en pude** *ehn poo·dher*
sheets	**lagener** *la·ner*
soap	**sæbe** *say·ber*
towels	**håndklæder** *hawn·klay·dhah*
Do you have lockers?	**Har I aflåste skabe?** *hah ee aw·lowsd·er ska·ber*
What time do you lock up?	**Hvornår lukker I for natten?** *voar·naw loa·gah ee foh nad·dern*
Do I need a membership card?	**Skal man have et medlemskort?** *skal man hah ehd medh·lems·kawd*
Here's my international student card.	**Her er mit internationale studiekort.** *hehr ehr meet in·tah·na·shoa·naleh stu·dyie·kawd*

Known as **DANHOSTEL, Danmarks Vandrerhjem**, the Danish Youth Hostel Association operates official youth hostels throughout Denmark. You may request a private or shared room. The charge covers only the cost of the room; additional fees apply for bed linens and/or breakfast. Hostelling International (HI) cardholders are exempt from surcharges and receive special discounts. HI membership cards can be purchased on the spot.

Going Camping

Can we camp here?	**Kan vi campere her?** *kan vee kahm·<u>peh</u>·ah hehr*
Is there a campsite near here?	**Er der en campingplads i nærheden?** *ehr dehr ehn <u>kahm</u>·ping·plas ee <u>nehr</u>·heh·dhern*
What is the charge per day/week?	**Hvad koster det per dag/uge?** *vadh <u>kohs</u>·dah deh pehr da/<u>oo</u>·er*
Are there...?	**Er der...?** *ehr dehr...*
cooking facilities	**køkkenfaciliteter** <u>kur</u>·ken·fa·see·lee·teh·dah
electrical outlets	**stikkontakter** <u>stik</u>·kohn·tahg·dah
laundry facilities	**vaskerum** <u>vas</u>·ger·roam
showers	**brusebad** <u>broo</u>·ser·badh
tents for hire	**telte til leje** <u>tehl</u>·der til <u>lie</u>·er
Where can I empty the chemical toilet?	**Hvor kan jeg tømme det kemiske toilet?** *voar kan yie <u>tur</u>·mer deh <u>keh</u>·mis·ger toa·ee·<u>lehd</u>*

For Domestic Items, see page 45

For In the Kitchen, see page 76.

YOU MAY SEE...

DRIKKEVAND	drinking water
CAMPING FORBUDT	no camping
BÅLTÆNDING/ GRILLNING FORBUDT	no fires/barbecues

Communications

ESSENTIAL

Where's an internet cafe?
Hvor ligger der en internetcafé? *voar li·gah dehr ehn in·tah·neht·ca·feh*

Can I access the internet here/check e-mail?
Kan jeg gå på internettet herfra/tjekke min e-mail? *kan yie gow paw in·tah·neh·derdh hehr·frah/tjay·ker meen ee·mail*

How much per hour/half hour?
Hvor meget koster det per time/halve time? *voar mie·erdh kohs·dah deh pehr tee·mer/hal·ver tee·mer*

How do I connect/log on?
Hvordan kobler/logger jeg mig på? *voar ·dan kohb·lah/lohg·ah yie mie paw*

I'd like a phone card, please.
Jeg vil gerne have et telefonkort, tak. *yie vil gehr·ner ha eht teh·ler·foan·kawd tahk*

Can I have your phone number?
Kan jeg få dit telefonnummer? *kan yie fow deet teh·ler·foan·noa·mer*

Here's my number/e-mail address.
Her er mit telefonnummer/min e-mail-adresse. *Hehr ehr meet teh·ler·foan·noa·mer/meen ee·mail·a·drah·ser*

Call me.	**Ring til mig.** *ring til mie*
E-mail me.	**Send mig en e-mail.** *sehn mie ehn ee·mail*
Hello. This is…	**Hallo. Det er…** *ha·loa deh ehr…*
I'd like to speak to…	**Jeg vil gerne tale med…** *yie vil gehr·ner ta·ler medh…*
Can you repeat that?	**Kan du gentage det?** *kan doo gehn·ta deh*
I'll call back later.	**Jeg ringer tilbage senere.** *yie ring·ah til·ba·yer seh·nah*
Bye.	**Farvel.** *fah·vehl*
Where's the post office?	**Hvor ligger posthuset?** *voar li·gah pohsd·hoo·serdh*
I'd like to send this to…	**Jeg vil gerne sende dette til…** *yie vil gehr·ner seh·ner deh·der til…*

Online

Where's an internet cafe?	**Hvor ligger der en internetcafé?** *voar li·gah dehr ehn in·tah·neht·ca·feh*
Does it have wireless internet?	**Har den trådløst internet?** *hah dehn trowdh·lurst in·tah·net*
What is the WiFi password?	**Hvad er WiFi-passwordet?** *vadh her WiFi·pass·word·edh*
Is the WiFi free?	**Er der gratis WiFi?** *ehr dehr ghra·tis WiFi*
Do you have bluetooth?	**Har I bluetooth?** *hahr ee bluetooth?*
How do I turn the computer on/off?	**Hvordan tænder/slukker jeg for computeren?** *voar·dan tay·nah/sloa·gah yie foh cohm·pew·dern*
Can I…?	**Kan jeg…?** *kan yie…*
access the internet here	**gå på internettet herfra** *gow paw in·tah·neh·derdh hehr· frah*

check e-mail	**tjekke min e-mail** _tjay_•ker meen _ee_•mail
print	**printe** _prin_•ter
plug in/charge my laptop/iPhone/iPad/BlackBerry?	**oplade min bærbare/iPhone/iPad/BlackBerry?** _ohb_•la•der meen _behr_•barer/iPhone/iPad/BlackBerry
access Skype?	**bruge Skype?** _broo_•er Skype
How much per hour/half hour?	**Hvor meget koster det per time/halve time?** _voar mie_•erdh _kohs_•dah deh pehr _tee_•mer/_hal_•ver tee•mer
How do I…?	**Hvordan….?** _voar_•_dan_…
connect/disconnect	**kobler jeg mig på/fra** _kohb_•lah yie mie paw/frah
log on/off	**logger jeg på/af** _lohg_•ah yie paw/a
type this symbol	**indtaster jeg dette symbol** _in_•tas•dah yie _deh_•der sewm•_boal_
What's your e-mail?	**Hvad er din e-mail adresse?** _vadh_ ehr deen _ee_•mail•a•drah•ser
My e-mail is…	**Min e-mail adresse er…** meen _ee_•mail•a•drah•ser ehr…
Do you have a scanner?	**Har I en scanner?** _hah_ ee ehn scan•ner

Social Media

Are you on Facebook/Twitter?	**Er du på Facebook/Twitter?** *her doo paw Facebook/Twitter*
What's your user name?	**Hvad er dit brugernavn?** *vadh ehr deet broo·er·nown*
I'll add you as a friend.	**Jeg vil tilføje dig som ven.** *yie vil til·foi·er die som vehn*
I'll follow you on Twitter.	**Jeg vil følge dig på Twitter.** *yie vil foil·ier die paw Twitter*
Are you following...?	**Følger du ...?** *foil·ier doo*
I'll put the pictures on Facebook/Twitter.	**Jeg vil lægge billederne op på Facebook/Twitter.** *yie vil lay·ger bee·leh·ar op paw Facebook/Twitter*
I'll tag you in the pictures.	**Jeg vil tagge dig på billederne.** *yie vil tag·ge die paw bee·leh·arner*

Phone

A phone card/prepaid phone, please.	**Jeg vil gerne have et telefonkort/ taletidskort, tak.** *yievil gehr·ner ha ehd teh·ler·foan·kawd/ ta·ler·teedhs·kawd tahk*

51

YOU MAY SEE…

E-MAIL	e-mail
FORLAD	exit
HJÆLP	help
INSTANT MESSENGER	instant messenger
INTERNET	internet
LOG IND	login
NY (BESKED)	new (message)
UDSKRIV	print
BRUGERNAVN/ADGANGSKODE	username/password
TRÅDLØS INTERNETFORBINDELSE	wireless internet

How much?	**Hvor meget koster det?** *voar <u>mie</u>·erdh <u>kohs</u>·dah deh*
Where's the pay phone?	**Hvor er mønttelefonen?** *voar ehr murnhd·teh·ler·foan*
What's the area/ country code for...?	**Hvad er områdenummeret/landekoden for...?** *vadh ehr <u>ohm</u>·row·dhe·noa·mahrdh/ <u>la</u>·ner·koa·dher foh...*
What's the number for Information?	**Hvad er nummeret til nummeroplysningen?** *Vadh ehr <u>noa</u>·mahrdh til <u>noa</u>·mah·ohb·<u>lews</u>·ning·ern*
I'd like the number for...	**Jeg vil gerne bede om nummeret til...** *yie vil <u>gehr</u>·ner beh ohm <u>noa</u>·mahrdh til...*
I'd like to call collect [reverse the charges].	**Jeg vil gerne ringe med modtager betaler.** *yie vil gehr·ner ring·er medh moadh·ta·ehr beh·ta·lar*
My phone doesn't work here.	**Min telefon virker ikke her.** *meen teh·ler·<u>foan</u> <u>veer</u>·gah ig·ger hehr*
What network are you on?	**Hvilket netværk er du på?** *vil·gerdh net·vehrk ehr doo paw*
Is it 3G?	**Er det 3G?** *ehr deh 3G*
I have run out of credit/minutes.	**Jeg har ikke mere taletid.** *yie hah ig·ger meh·rah ta·ler·teedh*

YOU MAY HEAR...

Hvem er det? *vehm ehr deh* — Who's calling?

Vær rar og vent. *vehr rah ow vehn·der* — Hold on.

Han/Hun kan ikke komme til telefonen. *han/hoon kan ig·ger koh·mer til teh·ler·foa·nern* — He/She can't come to the phone.

Ønsker du at lægge en besked? *urn·sgah doo ad lay·ger ehn beh·skehdh* — Would you like to leave a message?

Kan han/hun ringe tilbage til dig? *kan han/hoon ring·er til·ba·yer til die* — Can he/she call you back?

Hvad er dit telefonnummer? *vadh ehr deet teh·ler·foan·noa·mah* — What's your number?

Can I buy some credit?	**Kan jeg købe taletidskort her?** *kan yie kur·ber ta·ler·teedhs·kawd hehr*
Do you have a phone charger?	**Har du en telefonoplader?** *hah doo ehn te·ler·foan·op·la·dher*
Can I have your number?	**Må jeg få dit nummer?** *mow yie fow deet noa·mah*
My number is…	**Mit nummer er…** *meet noa·mah ehr…*
Call me.	**Ring venligst til mig.** *ring vehn·leest til mie*
Text me.	**Send mig venligst en tekstbesked.** *sehn mie vehn·leest ehn tehkst·beh·skehdh*
I'll call you.	**Jeg ringer til dig.** *yie ring·ah til die*
I'll text you.	**Jeg sender dig en tekstbesked.** *yie sehn·ah die ehn tehkst·beh·skehdh*

For Numbers, see page 159

Telephone Etiquette

Hello. This is...	**Hallo. Det er...** *ha·loa deh ehr...*
I'd like to speak to...	**Jeg vil gerne tale med...** *yie vil gehr·ner ta·ler mehdh...*
Extension...	**Lokal...** *loa·kal...*
Speak louder/more slowly, please.	**Vær rar og tal lidt højere/lidt langsommere.** *vehr rah ow ta·ler lit hoi·ah/lit lang·sohm·ah*
Can you repeat that?	**Kan du gentage det?** *kan doo gehn·ta deh*
I'll call back later.	**Jeg ringer tilbage senere.** *yie ring·ah til·ba·yer seh·nah*
Bye.	**Farvel.** *fah·vehl*

In Denmark, public phones either accept coins or prepaid phone cards. For coin-operated phones, once the line is engaged — even if it is busy — your coin will not be returned, so start with a low denomination coin. Prepaid phone cards can be purchased in post offices and kiosks. The price per call from a public phone is twice that from a private line but some kiosks allow you to make calls with a cheaper international rate using prepaid phone cards. Calls can also be made from the TelecomCenter at Central Train Station in Copenhagen. Important telephone numbers:

emergencies, 112
information, 118
operator assistance, 113

To call the U.S. or Canada from Denmark, dial 00 + 1 + area code + phone number. To call the U.K., dial 00 + 44 + area code (minus the first 0) + phone number.

Fax

Can I send/receive a fax here?	**Kan jeg sende/modtage en fax her?** *kan yie <u>sehn</u>•ner/<u>moadh</u>•ta ehn fahks hehr*
What's the fax number?	**Hvad er faxnummeret?** *vadh ehr fahks•noa•mahrdh*
Fax this to…	**Fax venligst dette til…** *fahks <u>vehn</u>•leesd <u>deh</u>•ter til…*

Post

Where's the post office/mailbox?	**Hvor ligger posthuset/er postkassen?** *voar li•gah <u>pohst</u>•hoo•serdh/ehr <u>pohst</u>•ka•sern*
A stamp for this letter/ postcard, please.	**Jeg vil gerne have et frimærke til dette brev/postkort, tak.** *Yie vil <u>gehr</u>•ne ha eht <u>free</u>•mehr•ker til <u>deh</u>•der brehw/<u>pohst</u>•kawd tahk*
How much?	**Hvor meget koster det?** *voar <u>mie</u>•erdh <u>kohs</u>•dah deh*
I'd like to send this package by airmail/ express.	**Jeg vil gerne sende denne pakke med luftpost/ekspres.** *yie vil <u>gehr</u>•ner <u>sehn</u>•ner <u>deh</u>•ner pah•ker mehdh <u>loaft</u>•pohst/ehks•<u>prehs</u>*
Can I have receipt?	**Kan jeg få en kvittering?** *kan yie fow ehn kvee•<u>teh</u>•ring*

The regular hours of operation of post offices in Denmark are Monday to Friday from 10:00 a.m. to 5:30 p.m. and Saturday 10:00 a.m. to 1:00 p.m.; hours in the provinces may vary. Mailboxes are red and, like post office signs, display an embossed crown-and-arrow logo and **POST** in white.

Food & Drink

VAN HAUEN BRØD
PR. 100 GRAM

7⁰⁰

ESSENTIAL

Can you recommend a good restaurant/bar? **Kan du anbefale en god restaurant/bar?** *kan doo an·beh·fa·ler ehn goadh reh·stoa·rang/bah*

Is there a traditional Danish/an inexpensive restaurant nearby? **Ligger der en typisk dansk/ikke så dyr restaurant i nærheden?** *li·gah dah ehn tew·peesk dansk/ig·ger saw dewr reh·stoa·rang ee nehr·heh·dhern*

A table for..., please. **Et bord til...tak.** *eht boar til...tahk*

Can we sit...? **Må vi sidde...?** *mow vee si·dher...*

here/there **her/der** *hehr/dehr*

outside **udenfor** *oo·dhern·foh*

at a non-smoking table **ved et bord for ikke-rygere** *vehdh eht boar foh ig·ger·rew·ah*

I'm waiting for someone. **Jeg venter på nogen.** *yie vehn·dah paw noa·ern*

Where are the toilets? **Hvor er toilettet?** *voar her toa·ee·leh·derdh*

I'd like a menu, please. **Jeg vil gerne bede om et menukort, tak.** *yie vil gehr·ner beh ohm eht meh·new·kawd tahk*

What do you recommend? **Hvad kan du anbefale?** *vadh kan doo an·beh·fa·ler*

I'd like... **Jeg vil gerne have...** *yie vil gehr·ner ha...*

Some more, please. **Jeg vil gerne have lidt mere, tak.** *yie vil gehr·ner ha lit meh·ah tahk*

Enjoy your meal. **Velbekomme.** *vehl·beh·koh·mer*

Can I have the check [bill]? **Kan jeg få regningen?** *kan yie fow rie·ning·ern*

Is service included?	**Er drikkepenge inkluderet?** *ehr drig·ger·pehng·er in·kloo·d**eh**·rerdh*
Can I pay by credit card?	**Kan jeg betale med kreditkort?** *kan yie beh·t**a**·ler mehdh kreh·deet·kawd*
Can I have a receipt?	**Kan jeg få en kvittering?** *kan yie fow ehn kvee·t**eh**·ring*
Thank you.	**Tak.** *tahk*

Where to Eat

Can you recommend…?	**Kanduanbefale…?** *kan dooan·beh·f**a**·ler…*
a restaurant	**en restaurant** *ehn reh·stoa·rang*
a bar	**en bar** *ehn b**a**h*
a cafe	**en café** *ehn ca·f**eh**_
a fast-food place	**en burgerbar** *ehn b**ur**·gah·bah*
a cheap restaurant	**en billig restaurant** *ehn bee·lee res·taw·rangh*
an expensive restaurant	**en dyr restaurant** *ehn dewr res·taw·rangh*
a restaurant with a good view	**en restaurant med god udsigt** *ehn res·taw·rangh medh gohd oodh·sight*
an authentic/ a non-touristy restaurant	**en autentisk/ikke-turistet restaurant** *ehn aw·ten·tisk/ig·ger tuh·rist·ehd res·taw·rangh*

Reservations & Preferences

I'd like to reserve a table…	**Jeg vil gerne bestille et bord…** *yie vil gehr·ner beh·stil·ler eht boar…*
for two	**til to** *til toa*
for this evening	**til i aften** *til ee ahf. tern*
for tomorrow at…	**til i morgen klokken…** *til ee mawn kloh·gehrn…*

A table for two, please. **Et bord til to, tak.** *eht boar til toa tahk*

We have a reservation. **Vi har en reservation.** *vee hah ehn reh•sah•va•shoan*

My name is... **Mit navn er...** *meet nown ehr...*

Can we sit...? **Må vi sidde...?** *mow vee si•dher...*

   here/there   **her/der** *hehr/dehr*

   outside   **udenfor** *oo•dhern•foh*

   at a non-smoking table   **ved et bord for ikke•rygere** *vehdh eht boar for ig•ger•rew•ah*

   by the window   **ved vinduet** *vehdh vin•doo•erdh*

   in the shade   **i skyggen** *ee skewg•gehn*

   in the sun   **i solen** *ee sohl•ehn*

Where are the toilets? **Hvor er toilettet?** *voar ehr toa•ee•leh•derdh*

YOU MAY HEAR...

Har du bestilt et bord? *hah doo beh•stild eht boar* — Do you have a reservation?

Til hvor mange? *til voar mang•er* — For how many?

Ryger eller ikke•ryger? *rew•ah ehl•lah ig•ger rew•ah* — Smoking or non-smoking?

Er I klar til at bestille? *ehr ee klah til ad beh•stil•ler* — Are you ready to order?

Hvad kunne I tænke jer? *vadh koo•ner ee tehn•ker yehr* — What would you like?

Jeg kan anbefale... *yie kan an•beh•fa•ler....* — I recommend...

Velbekomme. *vehl•beh•koh•mer* — Enjoy your meal.

Moms (sales tax or value-added tax) and service charges are already included in your final bill in restaurants. Tips for outstanding service are a matter of personal choice.

How to Order

Waiter/Waitress!	**Tjener/Frøken!** *tyeh·nah/frur·kern*
We're ready to order	**Vi er klar til bestille.** *vee ehr klah til ad beh·stil·ler*
May I see the wine list?	**Må jeg bede om en vinliste?** *mow yie beh ohm ehn veen·lis·der*
I'd like…	**Jeg vil gerne have…** *yie vil gehr·ner ha…*
a bottle of…	**en flaske…** *ehn flas·ger…*
a carafe of…	**en karaffel…** *ehn ka·rah·ferl…*
a glass of…	**et glas…** *eht glas…*
Can I have a menu?	**Må jeg bede om et menukort?** *mow yie beh ohm eht meh·new·kawd*
Do you have…?	**Er der…?** *ehr dehr…*
a menu in English	**et menukort på engelsk** *eht meh·new·kawd paw ehng·erlsk*
a fixed·price menu	**et dagens tilbud** *eht da·erns til·boodh*
a children's menu	**en børnemenu** *ehn bur·ner·meh·new*
What do you recommend?	**Hvad kan du anbefale?** *vadh kan doo an·beh·fa·ler*
What's this?	**Hvad er det?** *vadh ehr deh*
What's in it?	**Hvad er der i?** *vadh ehr da ee*
Is it spicy?	**Er det krydret?** *ehr deh krewdh·rerdh*
I'd like…	**Jeg vil gerne have…** *yie vil gehr·ner ha…*
More…please.	**Mere…tak.** *meh·ah…tahk*
With/Without…	**Med/Uden…** *mehdh/oo·dhern…*
I can't eat…	**Jeg må ikke spise…** *yie mow ig·ger spee·ser…*

rare	**letstegt** *leht·stehgt*
medium	**medium** *m<u>eh</u>·dee·oam*
well·done	**gennemstegt** *geh·nerm·stehgt*
It's to go [take away].	**Jeg tager det med mig.** *yie tah deh mehdhmie*

For Drinks, see page 77.

Cooking Methods

baked	**bagt** *bahgt*
boiled	**kogt** *kohgt*
braised	**grydestest** *gr<u>ew</u>·dher·stehgt*
breaded	**paneret** *pa·n<u>eh</u>·rerdh*
creamed	**tilberedt med fløde** *til·beh·rehd mehdh fl<u>ur</u>·dher*
diced	**skåret i terninger** *sk<u>aw</u>·rerdh ee t<u>eh</u>r·ning·ah*
fileted	**fileteret** *fee·leh·t<u>eh</u>·rerdh*
fried	**stegt** *stehgt*
grilled	**grillet** *gree·lerdh*
poached	**pocheret** *poa·sh<u>eh</u>·rerdh*
roasted	**ovnstegt** *own·stehgt*
sautéed	**sauteret** *saw·t<u>eh</u>·rerdh*
smoked	**røget** *roi·erdh*
steamed	**dampet** *dahm·berdh*
stewed	**stuvet** *st<u>oo</u>·erdh*
stuffed	**farseret** *fah·s<u>eh</u>·rerdh*

Dietary Requirements

I'm...	**Jeg...** *yie...*
diabetic	**har sukkersyge** *hah soa·gah·s<u>ew</u>·er*
lactose intolerant	**er laktoseallergiker** *ehr lahk·t<u>oa</u>·ser·a·lehr·gee·gar*
vegetarian	**er vegetar** *ehr veh·geh·t<u>ah</u>*
vegan	**veganer** *veh·gah·nehr*
I'm allergic to...	**Jeg kan ikke tåle...** *yie kan ig·ger t<u>ow</u>·ler...*
I can't eat...	**Jeg kan ikke spise...** *yie kan ig ger sp<u>ee</u> ser...*

dairy	**mælkeprodukter**	*mehl·ker·proa·doag·dah*
gluten	**gluten**	*gloo·dern*
nuts	**nødder**	*nur·dhah*
pork	**svinekød**	*svee·ner·kurdh*
shellfish	**skaldyr**	*skal·dewr*
spicy foods	**krydret mad**	*krewdh·rerdh madh*
wheat	**hvede**	*veh·dher*
Is it halal/kosher?	**Er det halal/kosher?**	*ehr deh ha·lal/koh·sher*
Do you have...?	**Har I...?**	*hah ee...*
skimmed milk	**skummetmælk**	*skum·medh·mehlk*
whole milk	**sødmælk**	*surdh·mehlk*
soya milk	**soyamælk**	*soya·mehlk*

Dining with Children

Do you have children's portions?	**Serverer I mad i børneportioner?** *sehr·veh·ah ee madh ee bur·ner·poh·shoa·nah*
A highchair/child's seat, please.	**Jeg vil gerne bede om en høj stol/et barnesæde, tak.** *yie vil gehr·ner beh ohm ehn hoi stoal/eht bah·ner·say·dher tahk*
Where can I feed/change the baby?	**Hvor kan jeg made/skifte babyen?** *voar kan yie ma·dher/skeef·der bay·bee·ern*
Can you warm this?	**Kan du opvarme dette?** *kan doo ohb·vah·mer deh·deh*

For Traveling with Children, see page 138.

How to Complain

How much longer will our food be?	**Hvor lang tid tager det, før maden er klar?** *voar lahng teedh tah deh fur ma·dhern ehr klah*
We can't wait any longer.	**Vi kan ikke vente længere.** *vee kan ig·ger vehn·der layng·ah*
We're leaving.	**Vi går.** *vee gaw*
I didn't order this.	**Det har jeg ikke bestilt.** *deh hah yie ig·ger beh·stilt*

I ordered...	**Jeg bad om...** *yie badh ohm...*
I can't eat this.	**Jeg kan ikke spise det her.** *yie kan ig·ger spee·ser deh hehr*
This is too...	**Det her er for...** *deh hehr ehr foh...*
cold/hot	**koldt/varmt** *kohlt/vahmt*
salty/spicy	**saltet/krydret** *sal·terdh/krewdh·rerdh*
tough/bland	**sejt/har ingen smag** *sied/hahing·ern sma*
This isn't clean/fresh.	**Det her er ikke rent/frisk.** *deh hehr ehr ig·ger rehnt/frisk*

Paying

I'd like the check [bill].	**Må jeg bede om regningen.** *mow yie beh ohm rie·ning·ern*
We'd like to pay separately.	**Vi vil gerne betale hver for sig.** *vee vil gehr·ner beh·ta·ler vehr foh sie*
It's all together.	**Vi vil gerne betale samlet.** *vee vil gehr·ner beh·ta·ler sahm·lerdh*
Is service included?	**Er drikkepenge inkluderet?** *ehr drig·ger·pehng·er in·kloo·deh·erdh*
What's this amount for?	**Hvad dækker dette beløb?** *vadh day·gah deh·der beh·lurb*
I didn't have that.. I had...	**Det har jeg ikke bestilt. Jeg fik...** *deh hah yie ig·ger beh·stilt yie feek...*
Can I pay by credit card?	**Kan jeg betale med kreditkort?** *kan yie beh·ta·ler mehdh kreh·deet·kawd*
Can I have an itemized bill/a receipt ?	**Må jeg bede om en udspecificeret regning/en kvittering?** *mow yie beh ohm ehn oodh·speh·see·fee·seh·ahdh rie·ning/ ehn kvee·teh·ring*
That was a very good meal.	**Det var meget lækker mad.** *deh vah mie·erdh lehg·gah madh*
I've already paid.	**Jeg har allerede betalt.** *yie hah a·ler·redher beh·ta·lt*

Meals & Cooking

Breakfast

appelsinjuice *ah·berl·seen·djoos*   orange juice
appelsinmarmelade   orange marmalade
ah·berl·seen·mah·mer·la·dher
bacon og æg *bay·kohn ow ayg*   bacon and eggs
brød *brurdh*   bread
blødkogt/hårdkogt æg *blurdh·kohgd/*   soft-/hard-boiled egg
haw·kohgd ayg

grapefrugtjuice *grayb·froagt·djoos*   grapefruit juice
havregrød *how·rah grurdh*   oatmeal
honning *hoh·ning*   honey
kaffe... *kah·fer...*   coffee...
   kaffeinfri *kah·feh·een·free*   decaffeinated
   med mælk *mehdh mehlk*   with milk
   sort *soart*   black
(kold/varm) mælk *(kohl/vahm) mehlk*   (cold/hot) milk
omelet *oa·mer·leht*   omelet
pandekager *pa·ner·ka·yah*   pancakes
pølser *purl·sah*   sausage

Morgenmad (breakfast) is usually eaten quite early, since school and work often begin at 8:00 a.m. A typical breakfast includes buttered bread, **skæreost** (sliced cheese), creamy white cheese like Havarti, jam and coffee. **Frokost** (lunch) is often a simple meal of buttered bread and spreads. **Aftensmad** (dinner) begins at about 6:00 p.m. and is the main meal, as well as the only hot meal, of the day. Dinner may include several courses or may simply be a hearty soup followed by dessert.

ristet brød *ris·terdh brurdh*	toast
rundstykker *roan·stur·gah*	rolls
røræg *rur·ayg*	scrambled eggs
smør *smur*	butter
spejlæg *spiel·ayg*	fried eggs
skinke og æg *skin·ger ow ayg*	ham and eggs
syltetøj *sewl·der·toi*	jam
te med mælk/citron *teh mehdh mehlk/ see·troan*	tea with milk/lemon
varm chokolade *vahm shoa·koa·la·dher*	hot chocolate
yoghurt *yoo·goord*	yogurt

Appetizers

ansjoser *an·shoa·sah*	anchovies
artiskokker *ah·tees·koh·gah*	artichokes
aspargeshoveder *a·spahs·hoah·dhah*	asparagus tips
champignoner *sham·pin·yong*	mushrooms
fyldte tomater *fewl·der toa·ma·dah*	stuffed tomatoes
gåselever *gow·ser·lehw·ah*	goose liver
kaviar *ka·vee·ah*	caviar

(marineret/røget) makrel	(marinated/smoked)
(mah·ree·neh·rahdh/roi·erdh) ma·krehl	mackerel
muslinger *moos·ling·ah*	mussels
oliven (fyldte) *oa·lee·vern (fewl·der)*	(stuffed) olives
radiser *rah·dee·sah*	radishes
rollmops *rohl·mops*	pickled herring [rollmops]
røget/graved laks *roi·erdh/grah·verdh lahks*	smoked/cured salmon
salat *sa·lat*	salad
saltkød *sahlt·kurdh*	salted beef slices
sild med løg *seel mehdh loi*	herring with onion
sildesalat *see·ler·sa·lat*	herring salad
skinke *skin·ger*	ham
spegepølse *spi·er·purl·ser*	salami
østers *urs·dahs*	oysters
ål (i gelé) *owl (ee sheh·leh)*	(jellied) eel

Soup

aspargessuppe *a·spahs·soa·per*	asparagus soup
champisnonsuppe *sham·pin·yong·soa·per*	mushroom soup
frugtsuppe *froagt·soa·per*	dried fruit soup, served chilled or hot
gule ærter *goo·ler ehr·dah*	split-pea soup with salt pork
hønsekødsuppe *hurn·ser·kurdhs·soa·per*	chicken and vegetable soup
hummersuppe *hoa·mah·soa·per*	lobster chowder
klar suppe med boller og grønsager *klah soa·per mehdh boh·lah ow grurn·sa·yah*	vegetable soup with meatballs
kråsesuppe *krow·ser·soa·per*	sweet-sour chicken giblets soup
labskoves *lahb·sgows*	hearty stew made with beef, potatoes, carrots and onions
æblesuppe *ay·bler·soa·per*	apple soup

Soup is, on many occasions, a meal on its own. If you'd like to try a traditional soup, order **aspargessuppe** (asparagus soup), **gule ærter** (split-pea soup), **frugtsuppe** (fruit soup) or chicken soup **med boller** (with meatballs).

ægte skildpaddesuppe   turtle soup
ayg·der skil·pa·dher·soa·per

øllebrød *ur·ler·brurdh*   soup of rye bread cooked
                                        with Danish beer, sugar
                                        and lemon

Fish & Seafood

aborre *a·bohr*	perch
ansjoser *an·shoa·sah*	anchovies
ål (i gelé/røget) *owl (ee sheh·leh/roi·erdh)*	(jellied/smoked) eel
blåmuslinger *blaw·moos·ling·ah*	mussels
forel *foh·rehl*	trout
gedde *geh·dher*	pike
helleflynder *heh·ler·flur·nah*	halibut
hummer *hoa·mah*	lobster
karpe *kah·per*	carp
kaviar *ka·vee·ah*	caviar
krebs *krehbs*	crab
laks *lahks*	salmon
makrel *ma·krehl*	mackerel
piahvar *peeg·vah*	turbot
rejer *rie·ah*	shrimp [prawns]
rogn *rown*	roe
rødspætte *rurdh·spay·der*	plaice

sardiner *sah·dee·nah*	sardine
sild *seel*	herring
røget *roi·erdh*	smoked
i lage *ee la·yer*	marinated in brine
marineret *mah·ree·neh·rerdh*	marinated
skrubbe *skroa·ber*	flounder
store rejer *stoa·ah rie·ah*	jumbo shrimp [prawns]
stør *stur*	sturgeon
søtunge *sur·toang·er*	sole
torsk *tohsk*	cod
tunfisk *toon·fisk*	tuna
ørred *ur·erdh*	trout
østers *urs·dahs*	oysters
ål *owl*	eel

Meat & Poultry

and *an*	duck
bacon *bay·kohn*	bacon
blodpølse *bloadh·purl·ser*	black pudding
bøftartar *burf·tah·tah*	beef tartare
brisler *brees·lah*	sweetbreads
due *doo·er*	pigeon
dyrekød *dew·er·kurdh*	venison
fasan *fa·san*	pheasant
forloren skildpadde *foh·loarn skil·pa·dher*	'mock turtle': a very traditional Danish dish consisting of meat from a calf's head with meatballs and fish balls
frikadeller *fri·ka·deh·lah*	small meat patties
fårekød *faw·er·kurdh*	mutton

Smørrebrød (open-faced sandwiches), comprised of buttered rye bread and sliced meat or cheese, have been a part of Danish cuisine for a long time; however, the fancier, more elaborate **smørrebrød** eaten on festive occasions appeared only in the late 1800s. Today **smørrebrød** is topped with a variety of delicacies: mounds of shrimp, eel, smoked salmon, marinated or smoked herring, liver paste, roast beef or pork and steak tartare. The sandwich is then garnished with a number of other ingredients: raw onions, cress, scrambled eggs, egg yolk, radishes, chives and pickled cucumbers to name a few.

Many large restaurants serve **smørrebrød**. You can select a traditional combination such as **dyrlægens natmad** (liver paté, corned beef and aspic **smørrebrød**), **rullepølse** (spiced meat roll) or **stjerneskud** (fish and shrimp **smørrebrød**), or you can name the individual items that you prefer.

grisehoved/grisetæer *gree·ser·hoa·wedh/ gree·ser·tehr*	pig's head/feet
grydesteg *gr<u>ew</u>·dher·stie*	pot roast
gås *gows*	goose
hakkebøf *hah·ker·burf*	ground beef patty
hamburgerryg *hahm·boh·rurg*	smoked, salted pork with cucumber sauce
hare *h<u>ah</u>·rer*	hare
kalkun *kal·k<u>oo</u>n*	turkey
kalvebrissel *kal·ver·bree·serl*	veal cutlet
kalvekød *kal·ver·kurdh*	veal
kanin *ka·n<u>ee</u>n*	rabbit
koldt kødpålæg *kohlt kurdh·paw·laygh*	cold cuts

kylling *kew·ling*	chicken
kødboller *kurdh·boh·lah*	small meatballs, usually served in soup or with pasta
lam *lahm*	lamb
lever *leh·wah*	liver
leverpaté *leh·wah·pa·teh*	liver paté
medisterpølse *meh·dees·dah·purl·ser*	spiced pork sausage
oksehale *ohk·ser·ha·ler*	oxtail
oksekød *ohk·ser·kurdh*	beef
oksesteg *ohk·ser·stie*	roast beef
pattegris *pa·der·grees*	suckling pig
perlehøne *pehr·ler·hur·ner*	guinea fowl
pølse *purl·sah*	sausage
rensdyr *rehns·dewr*	reindeer
skinke *skin·ger*	ham
sprængt oksebryst *sprehngt ohk·ser·brurst*	boiled, salted brisket of beef
svinekød *svee·ner·kurdh*	pork
ung and *oang an*	duckling
vagtel *vahg·derl*	quail
vildsvin *veel·sveen*	wild boar

Vegetables & Staples

agurk *a·goork*	cucumber
artiskokker *ah·tees·koh·kah*	artichokes
asparges *a·spahs*	asparagus
aubergine *oa·behr·sheen*	eggplant [aubergine]
avocado *a·vo·ka·doa*	avocado
blandede urter *bla·ner·dher oor·dah*	mixed herbs
blomkål *blom·kowl*	cauliflower
...bønner *...bur·nah*	...beans
brune *broo·ner*	kidney

grønne *grur·ner*		green
hvide *vee·dher*		butter
broccoli *broh·koa·lee*		broccoli
brød *brurdh*		bread
franskbrød *frahnsk·brurdh*		white bread
fuldkornsbrød *fool·koarns·brurdh*		whole-grain bread
pumpernikkel-brød		pumpernickel bread
poom·pah·ni·kerl·brurdh		
rugbrød *roo· brurdh*		rye bread
brøndkarse *brurn·kah·ser*		watercress
champienoner *shahm·peen·yong·ah*		mushrooms
courgette *koor·sheh·ter*		zucchini [courgette]
græskar *grehs·kah*		pumpkin
gulerødder *goo·ler·rur·dhah*		carrots
hvidløg *veedh·loi*		garlic
ingefær *ing·er·fayr*		ginger
julesalat *yoo·ler·sa·lat*		endive [chickory]
kapers *ka·pers*		capers
kartofler *ka·tohf·lah*		potatoes
kastanjer *ka·stan·yah*		chestnuts
kål *kowl*		cabbage
linser *lin·sah*		lentils
løg *loi*		onions
majs *mies*		corn
mel *mehl*		flour
nudler *noodh·lah*		noodles
pasta *pa·sta*		pasta
peber *peh·wah*		pepper (spice)
peberfrugt *peh·wah·froagt*		peppers
peberrod *peh·wah·roadh*		horseradish
porrer *poa·rah*		leeks

Measurements in Europe are metric — and that applies to the weight of food too. If you tend to think in pounds and ounces, it's worth brushing up on what the equivalent is before you go shopping for fruit and veg in markets and supermarkets. Five hundred grams, or half a kilo, is a common quantity to order, and that converts to just over a pound (17.65 ounces, to be precise).

radiser *rah·dee·sah*	radishes
ris *rees*	rice
roer *roa·ah*	turnip
rosenkål *roa·sern·kowl*	Brussels sprouts
rødbeder *rurdh·beh·dhah*	beets [beetroot]
salat *sa·lat*	lettuce
selleri *seh·ler·ree*	celery
skalotteløg *ska·loh·der·loi*	shallot
spansk peber *spansk peh·wah*	pimiento pepper
spinat *spee·nat*	spinach
søde kartofler *sur·dher ka·tohf·lah*	sweet potatoes
tomater *toa·ma·dah*	tomatoes
ærter *ehr·dah*	peas

Fruit

abrikoser *ah·bree·koa·sah*	apricots
ananas *a·na·nas*	pineapple
appelsin *ah·berl·seen*	orange
banan *ba·nan*	banana
blommer *bloh·mah*	plums
blåbær *blaw·behrr*	blueberries
citron *see·troan*	lemon
dadler *dadh·lah*	dates

fersken *fehrs·ger n*	peach
figner *feey·nah*	figs
grapefrugt *grayb·froagt*	grapefruit
hasselnøddur *ha·serl·nurdh·ah*	hazelnuts
hindbær *hin·behr*	raspberries
jordbær *yoar·behr*	strawberries
jordnødder *yoar·nurdh·ah*	peanuts
kastanjer *ka·stan·yah*	chestnuts
kirsebær *keer·ser·behr*	cherries
lime *liem*	lime
mandarin *man·da·reen*	tangerine
mandler *man·lah*	almonds
melon *meh·loan*	melon
nektarin *nehk·tah·reen*	nectarine
pære *pay·rah*	pear
rabarber *rah·bah·bah*	rhubarb
rosiner *roa·see·nah*	raisins
solbær *soal·behr*	black currants
stikkelsbær *sti·gerls·behr*	gooseberries
tyttebær *tew·der·behr*	cranberries
valnødder *val·nur·dha*	walnuts
vandmelon *van·meh·loan*	watermelon
vindruer *veen·droo·ah*	grapes
æble *ay·bler*	apple

Cheese

danablu *da·na·bloo*	Danish blue cheese
danbo *dan·boa*	mild, firm cheese, sometimes with caraway seeds
elbo *ehl·boa*	hard cheese with a delicate taste

esrom *ehs•roam*		strong, slightly aromatic cheese
maribo *mah•ree•boa*		soft, mild cheese
molbo *mohl•boa*		rich and highly flavored
mycella *mew•seh•la*		similar to Danish blue cheese, but milder
ost *oast*		cheese
samsø *sahm•sur*		mild, firm cheese with a sweet, nutty flavor

Dessert

appelsinfromage *ah•berl•seen•froa•ma•sher*	orange mousse
bondepige med slør *boa•ner•pee•er mehdh slur*	'veiled countrymaid': bread crumbs, apple sauce, cream, sugar
brune kager *broo•ner ka•yah*	spicy, crispy cookies [biscuits] with almond
citronfromage *see•troan•froa•ma•sher*	lemon mousse
flødekage *flur•dher•ka•yer*	cream cake
fromage *froa•ma•sher*	mousse
is *ees*	ice cream
kage *ka•yer*	cake

YOU MAY HEAR...

Kan jeg hjælpe dig? *kan yie yehl•per die*	Can I help you?
Hvad skulle det være? *vadh skoo deh vay•ah*	What would you like?
Skulle der være andet? *skoo dah vay•ah a•nerdh*	Anything else?
Det bliver...kroner. *deh bleer...kroa•nah*	That's...kroner

In Denmark, there are a few supermarket chains in addition to many local markets located in every city and town. Not all supermarkets accept international credit cards; some accept only **Dankort** (the special Danish equivalent of credit and debit cards). So remember to bring cash when you go shopping for groceries.

karamelrand *kah·rah·mehl·rehn*	caramel custard
pandekager *pa·ner·ka·yah*	thin pancakes
rødgrød med fløde *rurdh·grurdh mehdh flur·dher*	fruit jelly served with cream
små pandekager *smow pa·ner·ka·yah*	fritters
småkager *smaw·ka·yer*	cookies [biscuits]
æblekage med rasp og flødeskum *ay·ble·ka·yer mehdh rahsp ow flur·dher·skoam*	layers of stewed apple and cookie crumbs topped with whipped cream

Sauces & Condiments

salt *salt*	salt
peber *pe·wer*	pepper
sennep *seh·nerp*	mustard
ketchup *ket·youp*	ketchup

At the Market

Where are the trolleys/baskets?	**Hvor er vognene/kurvene?** *voar ehr vow·ner·ner/koor·ver·ner*
Where is?	**Hvor er...?** *voar ehr...*
I'd like some of that/those.	**Jeg vil gerne have noget af det/nogle af dem.** *yie vil gehr·ner ha noa·erdh a deh/noa·ler a dehm*
Can I taste it?	**Må jeg smage det?** *mow yie sma·yer deh*
I'd like.	**Jeg vil gerne have...** *yie vil gehr·ner ha...*

YOU MAY SEE...

MINDST HOLDBAR TIL...	best if used by...
KALORIER	calories
FEDTFRI	fat free
OPBEVARES I KØLESKAB	keep refrigerated
SIDSTE SALGSDATO	sell by
EGNET FOR VEGETARER	suitable for vegetarians

a kilo/half-kilo of...	**et kilo/halvt kilo...** *eht k**ee**·loa/halt k**ee**·lo...*
a liter/half-liter of...	**en liter/halv liter...** *ehn lee·dah/hal lee·dah...*
a piece of.	**et stykke...** *eht stur·ger...*
a slice of.	**en skive...** *ehn sk**ee**·ver...*
More/Less than that.	**Mere/Mindre end det.** *m**eh**·ah/min·drah ehn deh*
How much?	**Hvor meget koster det?** *voar mie·erdh kos·dah deh*
Where do I pay?	**Hvor kan jeg betale?** *voar kan yie beh·t**a**·ler*
Can I have a bag?	**Kan jeg få en bærepose?** *kan yie fow ehn b**ay**·rah·p**oa**·ser*
I'm being helped.	**Jeg bliver ekspederet.** *yie blee·vah ehks·peh·d**eh**·rahdh*

For Conversion Tables, see page 164.

In the Kitchen

bottle opener	**oplukker** *ohb·loag·gah*
bowls	**skåle** *sk**ow**·ler*
can opener	**dåseåbner** *d**ow**·ser·ow·bnah*
corkscrew	**proptrækker** *prohb·treh·kah*
cups	**kopper** *koh·bah*
forks	**gafler** *gahf·lah*
frying pan	**stegepande** *stie·yer·pa·ner*
glasses	**glas** *glas*

knives	**knive** *knee·ver*
measuring cup/	**målekrus/måleske** *mow·ler·kroos/*
spoon	*mow·ler·skeh*
napkins	**servietter** *sehr·vee·eh·dah*
plates	**tallerkner** *ta·lehrk·nah*
pot	**gryde** *grew·dher*
saucepan	**kasserolle** *ka·ser·rohl·ler*
spatula	**spatel** *spa·derl*
spoons	**skeer** *skeh·ah*

77

Drinks

ESSENTIAL

May I see the wine list/drink menu?	**Må jeg se vinlisten/listen med drinks?** *mow yie seh veen·lis·tern/lis·tern mehdh drinks*
What do you recommend?	**Hvad kan du anbefale?** *vadh kan doo an·beh·fa·ler*
I'd like a bottle/glass of red/white wine.	**Jeg vil gerne bede om en flaske/et glas rødvin/hvidvin.** *yie vil gehr·ner beh ohm ehn flas·ger/eht glas rurdh·veen/veedh·veen*
The house wine, please.	**Hustes vin, tak.** *hoo·sets veen tahk*
Another bottle/glass, please.	**En flaske/Et glas mere, tak.** *ehn flas·ger/eht glas meh·ah tahk*
I'd like a local beer.	**Jeg vil gerne bede om en lokal øl.** *yie vil gehr·ner beh ohm ehn loa·kal url*
Let me buy you a drink.	**Lad mig byde dig på en drink.** *ladh mie bew·dher die paw ehn drink*
Cheers!	**Skål!** *skowl*
A coffee/tea, please.	**En kop kaffe/te, tak.** *ehnkohpkah·fer/teh tahk*

With milk.	**Med mælk.** *mehdh mehlk*
With sugar.	**Med sukker.** *mehdh soa·gah*
With artificial sweetener.	**Med sødemiddel.** *mehdh sur·dher·mee·dherl*
. . .please.	**. . .tak.** . . .*tahk*
juice	**Juice** *djoos*
soda	**Sodavand** *soa·da·van*
sparkling/still water	**Danskvand/Kildevand** *dansk·van/kee·ler·van*

Non-alcoholic Drinks

appelsinjuice *ah·berl·seen·djoos*	orange juice
grapefrugtjuice *grayb·froagt·djoos*	grapefruit juice
kaffe *kah·fer*	coffee
limonade *li·moh·na·dher*	lemonade
mineralvand *mee·neh·rahl·van*	mineral water
mælk *mehlk*	milk
te *teh*	tea
tomatjuice *toa·mat·djoos*	tomato juice
varm chokolade *vahm shoa·koa·la·dher*	hot chocolate
æblejuice *ay·bler·djoos*	apple juice

If you're not in the mood for Danish beer, there are a number of other drinks to enjoy. Strong filtered coffee is enjoyed throughout the day, even with meals. If you prefer tea, herbal tea is growing in popularity. **Varm chokolade** (hot chocolate) is often served to children, but is also enjoyed by adults. For a unique drink, you could try **hyldeblomstsaft** (elderflower juice), a delicacy that is making a comeback. Or, if you simply prefer water, try **danskvand** or **mineralvand** (sparking or mineral water) with a bit of citrus fruit.

YOU MAY HEAR...

Må jeg byde på en drink?
mow yie bew•dher paw ehn drienk

Can I get you
a drink?

Med mælk eller sukker? *medh mehlk
ehl•er sug•gar*

With milk or sugar?

Vand meller eller uden brus?
van medh ehl•er udhen bruus

Sparkling or still
water?

Aperitifs, Cocktails & Liqueurs

akvavit *ah•kva•veet*	aquavit
aperitif *ah•peh•ree•teef*	aperitif
cognac *kon•yahk*	brandy
gin *djin*	gin
kalvados *kal•va•d<u>oh</u>s*	apple brandy
kirsebærcognac *keer•se•bayr•kon•yahk*	cherry brandy
likør *lee•kur*	liquer
portvin *poart•veen*	port wine
rom *rohm*	rum
snaps *snahps*	schnapps
vermouth *vehr•moot*	vermouth

Akvavit is a very popular drink in Denmark. Like vodka, it's
distilled from potatoes, though barley is also used. The color varies
according to the herbs and spices with which the drink is flavored.
Often served with a beer chaser, **akvavit** is drunk ice-cold, and makes
an ideal accompaniment to Danish appetizers.

vodka *vohd·ka* — vodka
...whisky *...wis·keei* — ...whisky
   tør *tur* — neat (straight)
   med isterninger *mehdh ees·tehr·ning·ah* — on the rocks
   med lidt vand *mehdh lit van* — with a little water
   med soda *mehdh soa·da* — with soda water

The Carlsberg and Tuborg breweries are internationally known; however, Denmark has many microbreweries that offer a variety of refreshing beer options. If you feel like trying something new, taste one of the local brews.

A special event every year is **J-day**, whose name comes from the Danish word **Juleøl** (Christmas beer). **J-day** is normally celebrated the first Friday in November, when, at exactly 8:59 p.m., all the Danish breweries release their special, limited edition Christmas beer. Each company creates a new recipe each year. That evening you'll find pubs filled with people enjoying their first beer of the Christmas season. **Skål!** (Cheers!)

Beer

En flaske... *ehn flas·ger...*	A bottle of...
En pilsner, tak. *ehn pils·nah tahk*	A pilsner, please.
Et glas... *eht glas...*	A glass of...
fadøl *fadh·url*	draft [draught] beer
udenlandsk øl *oo·dhern·lansk url*	imported beer
lys/mørk øl *lews/murrk øl*	light/dark beer
alkoholfri *øl alkho·hohl·free urhl*	non-alcoholic beer

Wine

...vin *...veen*	...wine
hvid *veedh*	white
mousserende *moo·seh·rern·der*	sparkling
rosé *roa·seh*	rosé
rød *rurdh*	red
sød *surdh*	sweet
tør *tur*	dry
champagne *cham·pan·ye*	champagne
dessertvin *des·serht·veen*	dessert wine
husets vin *hoo·serdhs veen*	house/table

On the Menu

aborre *ah·bohr*	perch
abrikoser *ah·bree·koa·sah*	apricots
afkølet *ow·kur·lerdh*	chilled
agerhøne *a·yer·hur·ner*	roast partridge served with red currant jam or apple sauce and horseradish
agurk *a·goork*	cucumber
agurksalat *a·goork·sa·lat*	cucumber in vinegar dressing

ananas *a·na·nas*	pineapple
and *an*	duck
and, stegt *an stehgt*	roast duck stuffed with chestnuts or apples and prunes, served with olive or mushroom sauce
anisfrø *a·nees·frur*	aniseed
ansjoser *an·shoa·sah*	anchovies
aperitif *ah·peh·ree·teef*	aperitif
appelsin *ah·berl·seen*	orange
appelsinfromage *ah·berl·seen·froa·ma·sher*	orange mousse
appelsinmarmelade *ah·berl·seen·mah·mer·la·dher*	marmalade
appelsinsovs *ah·berl·seen·sows*	orange sauce
artiskokker *ah·tees·koh·gah*	artichokes
asier *a·shah*	pickled gherkins
asparges *a·spahs*	asparagus
aspargeshoveder *a·spahs·hoh·dhah*	asparagus tips
aspargessuppe *a·spahs·soa·per*	asparagus soup
aubergine *oaber·sheen*	eggplant [aubergine]
avocado *a·vo·ka·doa*	avocado
bacon *bay·kohn*	bacon
banan *ba·nan*	banana
basilikum *ba·see·lee·koam*	basil
bearnaisesovs *behr·nays·sows*	a cream sauce flavored with tarragon and vinegar
beef *ohk·ser·kurdh*	oksekød
blandede grøntsager *bla·ner·dher grun·sa·yer*	mixed vegetables
blandede urter *bla·ner·dher·oor·dah*	mixed herbs
blandet hors d'oeuvre *bla·nerdh ohr durv·rah*	assorted appetizers
blodpølse *bloadh·purl·sah*	black pudding

blomkål *blohm·kowl*	cauliflower
blommer *bloh·mah*	plums
blå foreller *blaw foa·reh lah*	poached trout, serve with boiled potatoes, melted butter, horseradish and lemon
blåbær *blaw·behr*	blueberries
blåmuslinger *blaw·moos·ling·ah*	mussels
boller i karry *boh·lah ee kah·ree*	meatballs in a curry sauce
bondepige med slør *boh·ner·pee·yermehdh slur*	'veiled country maid': a mixture of bread crumbs, apple sauce, cream and sugar
brisler *brees·lah*	sweetbreads
broccoli *broh·koa·lee*	broccoli
brun sovs *broon sows*	traditional thick gravy
brune kager *broo·ner ka·yah*	spicy, crisp cookies [biscuits] with almonds
brunede kartofler *broo·ner·dher ka·tohf·lah*	caramelized potatoes
brød *brurdh*	bread
brøndkarse *brurn·kah·ser*	watercress
burger *bur·gah*	burger
bøftartar *burf·tah·tah*	beef tartare
bønner *bur·nah*	beans
champignoner *shahm·peen·yohng·ah*	mushrooms
champignonsuppe *sham·peen·yohng·so·per*	mushroom soup
chili *tjee·lee*	chili
(varm) chokolade *(vahm) shoa·koa·la·dher*	(hot) chocolate
chokoladeis *shoa·koa·la·dher·ees*	chocolate ice cream
chutney·smør *tjoht·nee smur*	chutney butter
citron *see·troan*	lemon
citronfromage *see·troan·froa·ma·sher*	lemon mousse

citronmarinade *see·tr<u>oa</u>n·mah·ree·na·dher*	marinade of lemon, oil, salt and pepper, paprika, herbs
citronsaft *see·tr<u>oa</u>n·sahft*	lemon juice
cognac *kohn·yahk*	cognac
courgette *koor·sheh·der*	zucchini [courgette]
dadler *dadh·lah*	dates
danablu *d<u>a</u>·na·bloo*	Danish blue cheese
danbo *dan·boa*	a mild, firm cheese, sometimes with caraway seeds
desserter *deh·sehr·tah*	desserts
dild *deel*	dill
drikkevarer *drig·ger·vah·rah*	beverages
due *d<u>oo</u>·er*	pigeon
dyrekød *d<u>ew</u>·rer·kurdh*	venison
dyreryg *d<u>ew</u>·rer·rurg*	saddle (cut of meat)
eddike *eh·dhee·ker*	vinegar
elbo *ehl·boa*	a hard cheese with a delicate taste
engelsk bøf *ehng·erlsk burf*	fillet of beef with onions and boiled potatoes
esrom *ehs·roam*	a strong, slightly aromatic cheese of spongy texture
estragon *eh·strah·gong*	tarragon
fadøl *fadh·url*	draft [draught] beer
fasan *fa·s<u>a</u>n*	pheasant
fennikel *feh·nee·kerl*	fennel
fersken *fehrs·gern*	peach
figner *f<u>ee</u>y·nah*	figs
fisk *fisk*	fish
fjerkræ *fyehr·kray*	poultry

flaskeøl *flas·ger·url*	bottled beer
flæskesteg med svær *flay·sger·stie mehdh svehr*	roast pork with crackling
flødekage *flur·dher·ka·yer*	cream cake
flødepeberrod *flur·dher·peh·wah·roadh*	horseradish cream dressing
forel *foa·rehl*	trout
forloren skildpadde *foh·loh·rern skil·pa·dher*	'mock turtle': a very traditional Danish dish consisting of meat, meatballs and fish balls
franskbrød *frahnsk·brurdh*	white bread
frikadeller *fri·ka·dehl·lah*	meatballs
fromage *froa·ma·sher*	mousse
frugt *froagt*	fruit
frugtsuppe *froagt·soa·per*	fruit soup, composed of a variety of dried fruits, served chilled or hot
fuldkornsbrød *fool·koarns·brurdh*	whole-grain bread
fyldte tomater *fewl·der toh·ma·dah*	stuffed tomatoes
fårekød *faw·er·kurdh*	mutton
gedde *geh·dher*	pike
gin *djin*	gin
grapefrugt *grayb·froagt*	grapefruit
grillstegt kylling *greel·stehgt kew·ling*	barbecued chicken
grisehoved *gree·ser·ho·wedh*	pig's head
grisetæer *gree·ser·tehr*	pig's feet
grydedesteg *grew·dher·stie*	pot roast
græskar *grehs·kah*	pumpkin
grønne bønner *grurn·ner bur·nah*	green beans
grøntsager *grurn·sa·yah*	vegetables
gule ærter *goo·ler ehr·dah*	split-pea soup with salt pork

gulerødder *goo•ler•rur•dhah*   carrots

gås *gows*   goose

gåselever *g<u>ow</u>•ser•leh•wah*   goose liver

hakkebøf *hah•ger•burf*   beef patties

hamburgerryg *hahm•boh•rurg*   smoked, salted saddle of pork, roasted and served in thin slices with Cumberland (cucumber-based) sauce

hare *h<u>ar</u>•rer*   hare

hasselnødder *ha•serl•nur•dhah*   hazelnuts

havregrød *how•er•grurdh*   porridge

helleflynder *heh•ler•flew•nah*   halibut

hindbær *hin•behr*   raspberries

honning *hoh•ning*   honey

hummer *hoa•mah*   lobster

hummersuppe *hoa•mah•soa•per*   lobster chowder

hvidløg *veedh•loi*   garlic

hvidvinssovs *veedh•veens•sows*   white wine sauce

hønsekødsuppe *hurn•ser•kurdhs•soa•per*   chicken and vegetable soup

hårdkogt *h<u>aw</u>•kohgtt*   hard-boiled

ingefær *ing•er•fehr*   ginger

is *ees*   ice cream

italiensk salat *ee•tal•y<u>eh</u>nsk sa•l<u>a</u>t*   diced carrots and asparagus, green peas and mayonnaise

jordbær *yoar•behr*   strawberries

jordbæris *yoar•behr•ees*   strawberry ice cream

jordnødder *yoar•nur•dhah*   peanuts

juice *djoos*   juice

julesalat *y<u>oo</u>•ler•sa•l<u>a</u>t*   endive

kaffe *kah•fer*   coffee

kaffeinfri *kah•feh•<u>een</u>•free*   decaffeinated

kage *ka·yer*	cake
kalkun *kal·koon*	turkey
kalkunragout *kal·koon rah·goo*	turkey in a sweet-and-sour gravy, served with mashed potatoes or a chestnut purée
kalvebrissel *kal·ver·bris·serl*	calf's sweetbread
kalvekød *kal·ver·kurdh*	veal
kanel *ka·nehl*	cinnamon
kanin *ka·neen*	rabbit
kanin i flødepeberrod *ka·neen ee flur·dher·peh·wah·roadh*	rabbit stew with horseradish cream dressing, roast mushroom and onions
kapers *ka·pahs*	capers
karaffel *ka·rah·ferl*	carafe
karamelrand *kah·rah·mehl·ran*	caramel custard
karpe *kah·per*	carp
kartoffel croquettes *ka·toh·ferl kroa·keh·dah*	potato croquettes
kartoffelmos (med æbler) *ka·toh·ferl·moas (mehdh ay·blah)*	mashed potatoes (with apple purée)
kartoffelsalat *ka·toh·ferl·sa·lat*	potato salad
kartofler *ka·tohf·lah*	potatoes
kastaniesovs *ka·stan·yer·sows*	chestnut sauce
kastanjer *ka·stan·yah*	chestnuts
kaviar *ka·vee·ah*	caviar
kirsebær *keer·ser·behr*	cherries
kirsebærcognac *keer·se·bayr·kohn·yahk*	cherry brandy
klar suppe med boller og grønsager *klah soa·per mehdh boh·lah ow grurn·sa·yah*	vegetable soup with meatballs
kokosnød *koa·kohs·nurdh*	coconut
koldt bord *kohlt boar*	smorgasbord
koldt kødpålæg *kolt kurdh·paw·laygh*	cold cuts

kommen *koh•mern*	cumin
kotelet *koa•der•leht*	chop, cutlet
krebs *krehbs*	crab
kryddernellike *kr**ew**•dher•neh•lee•ker*	clove
kråsesuppe *kr**ow**•ser•soa•per*	a sweet-sour chicken giblets soup, often with dried apples
kvæde *kv**ay**•dher*	quince
kylling *kew•ling*	chicken
kylling med rejer og asparges *kew•ling mehdh rie•ah ow a•sp**ah**s*	chicken in an asparagus sauce and garnished with shrimp
kyllingesalat *kew•ling•er•sa•l**at***	chicken, macaroni, tomato, peppers, olives, peas, lettuce and mushrooms, covered with a tomato dressing
kød *kurdh*	meat
kødboller *kurdh•boh•lah*	meatballs
labskovs *lahb•skows*	beef, diced potatoes, slices of carrots and onions, served with rye bread
lagkage *lahw•ka•yer*	layer cake
laks *lahks*	salmon
lam *lahm*	lamb
laurbærblad *lah•wer•behr•bl**a**•dher*	bay leaf
lever *leh•wah*	liver
likør *lee•kur*	liqueur
lime *liem*	lime
limonade *li•moa•n**a**•dher*	lemonade
linser *lin•sah*	lentils
lys hvidtøl *lews veed•url*	a pale, sweetish, low-alcohol beer
løg *loi*	onions

løgsovs *loi·sows* — onion sauce

majroer *mie·roa·ah* — turnips

majs *mies* — corn

makrel *ma·krehl* — mackerel

makrelsalat *ma·krehl·sa·lat* — mackerel in tomato sauce topped with mayonnaise

maltøl *malt·url* — a very heavy beer, regarded as a tonic

mandarin *man·da·reen* — tangerine

mandelgræskar *ma·nerl·grehs·kar* — vegetable marrow

mandler *man·lah* — almonds

maribo *mah·ree·boa* — a soft, mild cheese

marineret *mah·ree·neh·rerdh* — marinated

medisterpølse *meh·dees·dah·purl·sah* — spiced pork sausage, served with stewed vegetables or sautéed cabbage and potatoes

medium *meh·dee·oam* — medium

mel *mehl* — flour

melon *meh·loan* — melon

merian *meh·ree·an* — marjoram

milkshake *meelk·sjayk* — milkshake

mineralvand *mee·mer·rahl·van* — mineral water

molbo *mol·boa* — like Edam; a rich and highly flavored cheese

mousserende *moo·seh·rern·der* — sparkling (wine)

muskatnød *moo·skat·nurdh* — nutmeg

muslinger *moos·ling·ah* — mussels

mycella *mew·sehl·la* — similar to Danishblue cheese, but milder

mynte *mewn·der* — mint

mælk *mehlk*	milk
mørkt hvidtøl *murkt veed·url*	a dark beer; sweet and creamy
nektarin *nehk·tah·reen*	nectarine
nudler *noodh·lah*	noodles
nye kartofler *new·er ka·tohf·lah*	new potatoes
nyrer *new·rah*	kidneys
oksefilet *ohk·ser·fee·leh*	fillet
oksehale *ohk·ser·ha·ler*	oxtail
oksemørbrad *ohk·ser·mur·brahdh*	tenderloin
oksesteg *ohk·ser·stie*	roast beef
oksetyndsteg *ohk·ser·turn·stie*	sirloin
oliven (fyldte) *oa·lee·vern (fewl·der)*	olives (stuffed)
omelet *oa·mer·leht*	omelet
oregano *oh·reh·ga·noa*	oregano
ost *oast*	cheese
ovnstegt *own·stehght*	roast
pandekager *pa·ner·ka·yah*	pancakes
paprika *pahp·ree·ka*	paprika
pasta *pa·sta*	pasta
pattegris *pah·der·grees*	suckling pig
peber *peh·wah*	pepper (spice)
peberfrugt *peh·wah·froagt*	pepper (vegetable)
peberrod *pehr·wah·roadh*	horseradish
perlehøne *pehr·ler·hur·ner*	guinea fowl
persille *pehr·see·ler*	parsley
persillesovs *pehr·see·ler·sows*	parsley sauce
pighvar *peeg·vah*	turbot
pocheret æg *poa·sheh·rerdh ayg*	poached eggs
pommes frites *pohm freet*	French fries [chips]
porrer *poa·ah*	leeks

portvin *poart·veen*	port wine
pumpernikkel-brød *pohm·bah·ni·ker·brurdh*	pumpernickel bread
purløg *poor·loi*	chives
pære *pay·ah*	pear
pølse *purl·ser*	sausage
rabarber *rah·bah·bah*	rhubarb
radiser *rah·dee·sah*	radishes
ragout *ra·goo*	stew
rejer *rie·ah*	shrimp [prawns]
remoulade *reh·moa·la·dher*	mustard and herb cream dressing
rensdyr *rehns·dewr*	reindeer
ribbenssteg *ree·behns·stie*	ribsteak
rice *rees*	rice
ristet brød *ris·terdh brurdh*	toast
roer *roa·ah*	turnips
rogn *rown*	roe
rollmops *rol·mohps*	pickled herring [rollmops]
rom *rohm*	rum
rosé *roa·seh*	rosé
rosemarin *roas·mah·reen*	rosemary
rosenkål *roa·sern·kowl*	Brussels sprouts
rosiner *roa·see·nah*	raisins
rugbrød *roo·brurdh*	rye bread
rundstykker *roan·stur·gah*	rolls
rype *rew·per*	grouse
røget sild *roi·erdh seel*	smoked herring
røræg *rur·ayg*	scrambled eggs
rørt smør *rurt smur*	flavored cream butter
safran *sa·fran*	saffron
salat *sa·lat*	salad; lettuce

salt *salt*	salt
saltagurk *salt·a·goork*	pickles
saltkød *salt·kurdh*	salt beef slices
salvie *sal·vee·er*	sage
samsø *sahm·sur*	a mild, firm cheese with a sweet, nutty flavor
sardiner *sah·dee·nah*	sardines
selleri *seh·leh·ree*	celery
sellerisalat *seh·lebi·ree·sa·lat*	celery salad with a cheese dressing or mayonnaise
sellerisovs *seh·leh·ree·sows*	celery-flavored sauce with sherry
sennep *seh·nerp*	mustard
sennepssovs *seh·nerps·sows*	mustard sauce
sild *seel*	herring
sild i karry *seel ee kah·ree*	herring in curry sauce
sild med løg *seel mehdh loi*	herring with onion
sild, røget *seel roi·erdh*	herring, smoked, on dark rye bread, garnished with a raw egg yolk, radishes and chives
sildesalat *see·ler·sa·lat*	marinated or pickled herring, beet, apple and pickles in a spicy dressing
skaldyr *skal·dewr*	seafood
skalotteløg *ska·loh·ter·loi*	shallot
skank *skahnk*	shank
skibsøl *skeebs·url*	dark 'ship's beer' noted for its smoked-malt-character
skidne æg *skeedh·ner ayg*	poached or hard-boiled eggs in a cream sauce, with fish and mustard

skinke *skin·ger*	ham
skinke og æg *skin·ger ow ayg*	ham and eggs
skrubbe *skroa·ber*	flounder
smør *smur*	butter
smørrebrød *smur·er·brurdh*	famous Danish open-faced sandwich
små pandekager *smow pa·ner·ka·yah*	fritters
småkager *smow·ka·yah*	cookies [biscuits]
solbær *soal·behr*	black currants
spansk peber *spansk peh·wah*	pimiento pepper
spegepølse *spie·er·purl·ser*	salami
spejlæg *spiel·ayg*	fried eggs
spinat *spee·nat*	spinach
spiseolie *spee·ser·oal·yer*	oil
sprængt oksebryst *sprayngt ohk·ser·brurst*	boiled, salted beef brisket
spækket steg *speh·gerdh stie*	larded roast
stærk salatsovs *stehrk sa·lat·sows*	egg yolks, vinegar or lemon juice, oil, salt and pepper or paprika, Worcester sauce, onion or garlic and dill, all mixed with whipped cream
stegte kartofler *stehg·der ka·tohf·lah*	sautéed potatoes
stikkelsbær *sti·kerls·behr*	gooseberries
store rejer *stoa·ah rie·ah*	shrimp [prawns]
stør *stur*	sturgeon
sukker *soa·gah*	sugar
suppe *soa·pah*	soup
sylteagurker *sewl·der·a·goor·kah*	gherkins
syltetøj *sewl·der·toi*	jam
søde kartofler *sur·dher ka·tohf·lah*	sweet potatoes
sødemiddel *sur·dher·mee·dherl*	artificial sweetener

søtunge *sur·toang·ah*	sole
torsk *tohsk*	cod
torsk, kogt *tohsk kohgt*	cod, poached
torskerogn, ristet *tohs·ger·rown ris·terdh*	cod roe, fried
tunfisk *toon·fisk*	tuna
tunge *toang·er*	tongue
tyttebær *tew·der·behr*	cranberries
tørret frugt *tur·erdh froagt*	dried fruit
ung and *oang an*	duckling
vagtel *vahg·derl*	quail
valnødder *val·nur·dhah*	walnuts
vand *van*	water
vandmelon *van·meh·loan*	watermelon
vanilje *va·nil·yer*	vanilla
vegetar *veh·ger·tah*	vegetarian
vermouth *vehr·moot*	vermouth
vildsvin *veel·sveen*	wild boar
vildt *veelt*	game
vildtsovs *veelt·sows*	sauce of fresh cream and red currant jam
vin *veen*	wine
vinaigrette·sovs *vee·na·greht·sows*	vinegar and oil dressing
vindruer *veen·droo·ah*	grapes
vinkogt laks med pikant sovs *veen·kogt lahks mehdh pee·kant sows*	salmon poached in white wine, dressed with a spicy sauce
vodka *vohd·ka*	vodka
whisky *whis·kee*	whisky
ymersovs *ew·mah·sows*	lemon juice, spices and herbs, mixed with milk or cream
yoghurt *yoo·goord*	yogurt

æble _ay_-bler — apple

æbleflæsk _ay_-bler-flaysk — smoked bacon with onions and sautéed apple rings

æblekage med rasp og flødeskum _ay_-bler-**ka**-yer mehdh rahsp ow fl**ur**-dher-skoam — stewed apples with vanilla served with layers of cookie crumbs and topped with whipped cream

æblesuppe _ay_-bler-soa-per — apple soup

æg _ayg_ — egg

æggekage _ay_-ger-ka-yer — scrambled eggs with onions, chives, potatoes and bacon

æggesovs _ay_-ger-sows — egg sauce

æggeretter _ay_-ger-reh-dah — egg dishes

ægte skildpaddesuppe _ehg_-der skil-**pa**-dher-soa-per — turtle soup

øl _url_ — beer

øllebrød _ur_-lah-brurdh — rye bread cooked with Danish beer, sugar and lemon, served with milk and cream

ørred _ur_-rerdh — trout

østers _urs_-dahs — oysters

ål _owl_ — eel

ål, stegt med stuvede kartofler _owl stehg mehdh st**oo**-ver-dher ka-tof-lah — eel, fried, with diced potatoes in a white sauce

ålesuppe _ow_-ler-soa-per — sweet-and-sour eel soup, with apples and prunes, served with dark rye bread

People

Conversation

ESSENTIAL

Hello!	**Hej!** *hie*
How are you?	**Hvordan har du det?** *Voar·<u>dan</u> har doo deh*
Fine, thanks.	**Godt, tak.** *goht tahk*
Excuse me!	**Undskyld!** <u>oan</u>·*skewl*
Do you speak English?	**Kan du tale engelsk?** *kan doo <u>ta</u>·ler <u>ehng</u>·erlsk*
What's your name?	**Hvad hedder du?** *vadh <u>heh</u>·dhah doo*
My name is...	**Mit navn er...** *meet nown ehr...*
Nice to meet you.	**Det glæder mig at træffe dig.** *deh <u>glay</u>·dhah mie ad <u>treh</u>·fer die*
Where are you from?	**Hvor kommer du fra?** *voar <u>koh</u>·mah doo frah*
I'm from the U.S./ the U.K.	**Jeg kommer fra USA/England.** *yie <u>koh</u>·mah frah oo·ehs·a/ehng·lan*
What do you do?	**Hvad laver du?** *vadh <u>la</u>·vah doo*
I work for...	**Jeg arbejder hos...** *yie <u>ah</u>·bey·dah hohs...*
I'm a student.	**Jeg studerer.** *yie stoo·<u>deh</u>·rah*
I'm retired.	**Jeg er pensionist.** *yie ehr pang·shoa·<u>neest</u>*
Do you like...?	**Kan du lide...?** *kan doo lee...*
Goodbye.	**Farvel.** *fah·<u>vehl</u>*
See you later.	**På gensyn.** *paw <u>gehn</u>·sewn*

De (the formal form of you) is generally no longer used to address strangers, but is restricted to formal letters, addressing the elderly or addressing members of the royal family. As a general rule, **du** can be used in all situations without offending anyone.

Language Difficulties

Do you speak English?	**Kan du tale engelsk?**	*kan doo <u>ta</u>·ler <u>ehng</u>·erlsk*
Does anyone here speak English?	**Er der nogen her, der kan tale engelsk?**	*ehr dehr <u>noa</u>·ern hehr dehr kan <u>ta</u>·ler <u>ehng</u>·erlsk*
I don't speak (much) Danish.	**Jeg kan ikke tale (ret meget) dansk.**	*yie kan <u>ig</u>·ger <u>ta</u>·ler (reht <u>mie</u>·erdh) dansk*
Can you speak more slowly?	**Kan du tale lidt langsommere?**	*kan doo <u>ta</u>·ler lit <u>lang</u>·sohm·ah*
Can you repeat that?	**Kan du gentage det?**	*kan doo <u>gehn</u>·ta·yer deh*
What was that?	**Hvad var det?**	*vadh vah deh*
Can you spell it?	**Kan du stave til det?**	*kan doo stawe deh*
Please write it down.	**Vær rar og skriv det ned.**	*vehr rah ow skreew deh nedh*
Can you translate this for me?	**Kan du oversætte det her for mig?**	*kan doo <u>oh</u>·wah·seh·der deh hehr for mie*
What does this mean?	**Hvad betyder det her?**	*vadh beh·<u>tew</u>·dhah deh hehr*
I understand.	**Jeg forstår det godt.**	*yie foh·<u>staw</u> deh goht*
I don't understand.	**Jeg forstår det ikke.**	*yie foh·<u>staw</u> deh ig·ger*
Do you understand?	**Kan du forstå det?**	*kan doo foh·<u>staw</u> deh*

Making Friends

Hello!	**Hej!**	*hie*
Good morning.	**God morgen.**	*goadh·<u>mohn</u>*

YOU MAY HEAR...

Jeg taler kun lidt engelsk. *yie <u>ta</u>·lah koon lit <u>ehng</u>·erlsk*   I only speak a little English.

Jeg kan ikke tale engelsk. *yie kan <u>ig</u>·ger <u>ta</u>·ler <u>ehng</u>·erlsk*   I don't speak English.

Good afternoon.	**God eftermiddag.** *goadh·ef·tah·mi·da*
Good evening.	**God aften.** *goadh·ahf·tern*
My name is…	**Mit navn er…** *meet nown ehr…*
What's your name?	**Hvad hedder du?** *vadh heh·dhah doo*
Let me introduce you to…	**Lad mig præsentere dig for…** *ladh mie pray·sehn·teh·rer die foh…*
Nice to meet you.	**Det glæder mig at træffe dig.** *deh glay·dhah mie ad tray·fer die*
How are you?	**Hvordan har du det?** *voar·dan hah doo deh*
Fine, thanks.	**Godt, tak.** *goht tahk*
And you?	**Og hvordan har du det?** *ow voar·dan hah doo deh*

In Denmark, upon meeting, it is customary to shake hands for both men and women. Close friends (male-female/female-female) may give kisses on the cheeks. As a greeting, you could say **Går det godt?** (How's it going?) or **Hva så?** (What's up?). **Hej** is used both for hello or hi and bye.

Travel Talk

I'm here...	**Jeg er her...** *yie ehr hehr...*
on business	**på forretningsrejse** *pow foh·reht·nings·rie·ser*
on vacation [holiday]	**på ferie** *paw fehr·yer*
studying	**for at studere** *foh ad stoo·deh·er*
I'm staying for...	**Jeg skal være her...** *yie skal vay·ah hehr...*
I've been here...	**Jeg har været her...** *yie hah vay·erdh hehr...*
a day	**en dag** *ehn da*
a week	**en uge** *ehn oo·er*
a month	**en måned** *ehn mow·nerdh*
Where are you from?	**Hvor kommer du fra?** *voar koh·mah doo frah*
I'm from...	**Jeg kommer fra...** *yie koh·mah frah...*

For Numbers, see page 159.

Personal

Who are you with?	**Hvem er du her sammen med?** *vehm ehr doo hehr sah·mern mehdh*
I'm on my own.	**Jeg er her alene.** *yie ehr hehr a·leh·ner*
I'm with...	**Jeg er her sammen med...** *yie ehr hehr sah·mern mehdh...*
my husband/wife	**min mand/kone** *meen man/koa·ner*
my boyfriend/ girlfriend	**min kæreste** *meen kehr·sder*
a friend	**en ven** *ehn vehn*
a colleague	**en kollega** *ehn koa·leh·ga*
When's your birthday?	**Hvornår et det din fødselsdag?** *voar·naw ehr deh deen fur·sehls·da*
How old are you?	**Hvor gammel er du?** *voar gah·merl ehr doo*
I'm...	**Jeg er...** *yie ehr...*
Are you married?	**Er du gift?** *ehr doo geefd*

I'm...	**Jeg er...** *yie ehr...*
single	**ugift** *oo-geefd*
in a relationship	**i et seriøst forhold** *ee eht seh-ree-ursd foh-hohl*
engaged	**forlovet** *for-lowedh*
married	**gift** *geefd*
divorced	**skilt** *skild*
separated	**separeret** *seh-pah-reh-erdh*
I'm widowed.	**Jeg er enkemand** *m* **/enke** *f*. *yie ehr ehn-ker-man/ehn-ker*
Do you have children/ grandchildren?	**Har du nogen børn/børnebørn?** *hah doo noa-ern burn/bur-ner-burn*

For Numbers, see page 159.

Work & School

What do you do?	**Hvad laver du?** *vadh la-ver doo*
What are you studying?	**Hvad studerer du?** *vadh stoo-deh-ah doo*
I'm studying...	**Jeg studerer...** *yie stoo-deh-ah...*
I work full time/part time.	**Jeg arbejder fuldtids/deltids.** *Yie ah-bey-dah fool-teedhs/dehl-teedhs*

I work at home.	**Jeg arbejder hjemmefra.** *yie ah·bey·dah*
	yeh·mer·frah
I'm unemployed	**Jeg er arbejdsløs** *yie ehr arh·bieydhs·lurs*
Who do you work for?	**Hvor arbejder du henne?** *voar ah·bey·dah doo heh·ner*
I work for...	**Jeg arbejder hos...** *yie ah·bey·dah hohs...*
Here's my business	**Her er mit visitkort.** *hehr ehr meet*
card	*vee·seet·kawd*

For Business Travel, see page 135.

Weather

What's the weather	**Hvordan er vejrudsigten?** *voar·dan ehr*
forecast?	*vehr·oodh·sig·dern*
What beautiful/	**Hvor er det smukt/frygteligt vejr!** *voar ehr*
terrible weather!	*deh smoagt/frurg·ter·leed vayr*
It's...	**Det...** *deh...*
cold	**koldt** *kohldh*
cool	**er koldt** *ehr kohlt*
hot	**hot** *hodh*
icy	**er iskoldt** *ehr ees·kohlt*
rainy	**regner** *rie·nah*
snowy	**sner** *snehr*
warm	**er varmt** *ehr vahmt*
It's sunny.	**Solen skinner.** *soa·lern ski·nah*
Do I need a jacket/	**Har jeg brug for en jakke/paraply?** *hah yie*
an umbrella?	*broo foh ehn yah·ker/pah·rah·plew*

For Temperature, see page 165.

ESSENTIAL

Would you like to go out for a drink/meal ?	**Har du lyst til at gå ud og få en drink/noget at spise?** _hah doo lurst til ad gow ood ow fow ehn drink/noa·erdh ad spee·ser_
What are your plans for tonight/tomorrow ?	**Hvad er dine planer for i aften/i morgen?** _vadh ehr dee·ner pla·nah foh ee ahf·tern/ee mohn_
Can I have your number?	**Må jeg få dit nummer?** _mow yie fow deet noa·mah_
Can I join you?	**Må jeg komme med dig?** _mow yie koh·mer mehdh die_
Let me buy you a drink.	**Lad mig købe dig en drink.** _ladh mie kur·ber die ehn drink_
I like you.	**Jeg kan lide dig.** _yie kan lee die_
I love you.	**Jeg elsker dig.** _yie ehl-skah die_

The Dating Game

Would you like to go out…?	**Kunne du tænke dig at gå ud…?** _koon·ner doo tehnker die at gaw oodh_
for coffee	**og få en kop kaffe** _ow fow ehn kop kaf·eh_
for a drink	**og få en drink** _ow fow ehn drienk_
to dinner	**spise middag** _spee·ser mid·da_
What are your plans for…?	**Hvad er dine planer for…?** _vadh ehr dee·ner pla·nah foh…_
today	**i dag** _ee da_
tonight	**i aften** _ee ahf·tern_
tomorrow	**i morgen** _ee mohn_
this weekend	**weekenden** _vee·gehn·dern_

Where would you like to go?	**Hvor har du lyst til at gå hen?** *voar hah doo lurst til ad gow hehn*
I'd like to go to...	**Jeg vil gerne...** *yie vil <u>gehr</u>•ner...*
Do you like...?	**Har du lyst til at...?** *hah doo lurst til ad...*
Can I have your number/e-mail?	**Må jeg få dit nummer/din e-mail adresse?** *mow yie fow deet <u>noa</u>•mah/deen <u>ee</u>•mayl•a•drah•ser*
Are you on Facebook /Twitter?	**Er du på Facebook/Twitter?** *ehr doo paw Facebook/ Twitter*
Can I join you?	**Må jeg komme med dig?** *mow yie <u>koh</u>•mer mehdh die*
You're very attractive.	**Du er meget køn.** *doo ehr <u>mie</u>•erdh kurn*
Shall we go somewhere quieter?	**Skal vi gå hen et sted, hvor der er mere stille?** *skal vee gow hen eht stehdh voar dehr ehr <u>meh</u>•ah sti•ler*

For Conversation, see page 97.

Accepting & Rejecting

Thanks, I'd love to.	**Tak, det vil jeg meget gerne.** *tahk deh vil yie <u>mie</u>•erdh <u>gehr</u>•ner*
Where can we meet?	**Hvor skal vi mødes?** *voar skal vee <u>mur</u>•dhers*

I'll meet you at the bar/your hotel.	**Jeg møder dig i baren/på dit hotel.** *Yie mur·dhah die ee bahn/paw deet hoa·tehl*
I'll come by at...	**Jeg kommer klokken...** *yie koh·mah kloh·gehrn...*
What's your address?	**Hvad er din adresse?** *vadh ehr deen a·drah·ser*
Thank you, but I'm busy.	**Tak, men jeg er desværre optaget.** *tahk mehn yie ehr deh·svehr ohp·ta·erdh*
No thanks, I'm not interested.	**Nej tak, jeg er ikke interesseret.** *nie tahk yie ehr ig·ger in·trah·seh·erdh*
Leave me alone!	**Vær rar og lad mig være i fred!** *vehr rah ow la mie vay·er ee frehdh*
Stop bothering me!	**Lad mig være i fred!** *la mie vay·er ee frehdh*

Getting Intimate

Can I hug/kiss you?	**Må jeg kramme/kysse dig?** *mow yie krah·mer/kur·ser die*
Yes.	**Ja.** *ya*
No.	**Nej.** *nie*
Stop!	**Stop!** *Stohb*

Sexual Preferences

Are you gay?	**Er du homoseksuel?** *ehr doo hoa·moa·sehk·soo·ehl*
I'm...	**Jeg er...** *yie ehr...*
heterosexual	**heteroseksuel** *heh·teh·roa·sehk·soo·ehl*
homosexual	**homoseksuel** *hoa·moa·sehk·soo·ehl*
bisexual	**biseksuel** *bee·sehk·soo·ehl*
Do you like men/ women?	**Er du til mænd/kvinder?** *ehr doo til mehn/ kveen·ar*

Leisure Time

ESSENTIAL

Where's the tourist information office?	**Hvor ligger turistinformationen?** *Voar li·gah too·reest·in·foh·ma·shoa·nern*
What are the main points of interest?	**Hvad er de vigtigste seværdigheder?** *Vadh ehr dee vig·tee·ster seh·vehr·dee·heh·dhah*
Do you offer tours in English?	**Tilbyder I turer på engelsk?** *til·bew·dhah ee too·ah paw ehng·erlsk*
Can I have a map/ guide?	**Må jeg få et kort/en guidebog?** *mow yie fow eht kawd/ehn guide·bow*

Tourist Information

Do you have any information on...?	**Har du nogen information om...?** *hah doo noa·ern in·foh·ma·shoan ohm...*
Can you recommend...?	**Kan du anbefale...?** *kan doo an·beh·fa·ler...*
a boat trip	**en bådtur** *ehn bowdh·toor*
an excursion	**en udflugt** *ehn oodh·floagt*
a sightseeing tour	**en rundtur** *ehn roan·toor*

On Tour

I'd like to go on the tour to...	**Jeg vil gerne på turen til...** *yie vil gehr·ner paw too·ern til...*
When's the next tour?	**Hvornår starter den næste tur?** *voar·naw star·dah dehn nehs·der toor*
Are there tours in English?	**Er der ture på engelsk?** *ehr dehr too·ah paw ehng·erlsk*

Is there an English-speaking guide/audio guide?	**Er der en engelsktalende guide/engelsk lydguide?** *ehr dehr ehn ehng·erlsk·ta·ler·ner guide/ehng·erlsk lewdh·guide*
What time do we leave/return?	**Hvad tid tager vi afsted/kommer vi tilbage?** *vadh teedh tah vee a·stehdh/koh·mah vee til·ba·yer*
We'd like to see…	**Vi vil gerne se…** *vee vil gehr·ner seh…*
Can we stop here…?	**Kan vi stoppe her…?** *kan vee stoh·ber hehr…*
to take photographs	**for at tage billeder** *foh ad ta bil·ler·dhah*
to buy souvenirs	**for at købe souvenirs** *foh ad kur·ber sou·ve·neers*
to use the toilets	**for at gå på toilettet** *foh ad gow paw toa·ee·leh·derdh*
Is there access for the disabled?	**Er der adgang for handicappede?** *ehr dehr adh·gahng foh han·dee·kah·per·dher*

For Tickets, see page 20.

Tourist information offices are located throughout Denmark. The local tourist office can provide a wealth of information on accommodation, activities and other entertainment. An extensive list of all the tourist offices in Denmark can be found on Visit Denmark (www.visitdenmark.com), the Danish Tourist Board's website.

Seeing the Sights

Where is/are…?	**Hvor er…?** *voar ehr…*
the battleground	**kamppladsen** *kahmp·plas·sern*
the botanical gardens	**den botaniske have** *dehn boa·ta·nees·ker ha·ver*
the castle	**slottet** *sloh·derdh*

the downtown area	**den indre by** dehn <u>in</u>·drah bew
the fountain	**springvandet** <u>spring</u>·van·nerdh
the library	**biblioteket** beeb·lee·oa·<u>teh</u>·kerdh
the market	**torvet** <u>toh</u>·werdh
the museum	**museet** moo·<u>say</u>·erdh
the old town	**den gamle bydel** dehn gahm·ler <u>bew</u>·dehl
the opera house	**Operaen** ope·raehn
the palace	**slottet** <u>sloh</u>·derdh
the park	**parken** <u>pah</u>·gern
the ruins	**ruinerne** roo·<u>ee</u>·nah·ner
the shopping area	**indkøbscentret** <u>in</u>·kurbs·sehn·tahdh
the town square	**rådhuspladsen** <u>rawdh</u>·hoos·pla·sern
Can you show me on the map?	**Kan du vise mig det på kortet?** kan doo <u>vee</u>·ser mie mie deh paw kaw·derdh
It's…	**Det er…** deh ehr…
amazing	**forbløffende** foh·<u>blur</u>·fern·der
beautiful	**smukt** smoakt
boring	**kedeligt** <u>keh</u>·dher·leet
interesting	**interessant** in·trah·<u>sant</u>
magnificent	**storartet** <u>stoar</u>·ah·derdh

romantic	**romantisk** *roa•man•tisk*
strange	**underligt** *oa•nah•leet*
stunning	**fantastisk flot** *fan•tas•tisk floht*
terrible	**frygteligt** *frurg•ter•leet*
ugly	**grimt** *grimt*
I like/don't like it.	**Jeg kan lide/ikke lide det.** *yie kan lee/ ig•ger lee deh*

For Asking Directions , see page 34.

Religious Sites

Where's…?	**Hvor er…?** *voar ehr…*
the cathedral	**domkirken** *dohm•keer•gern*
the church	**kirken** *keer•gern*
the mosque	**moskeen** *moa•skeh•ern*
the shrine	**helgengraven** *hehl•yern•grah•vern*
the synagogue	**synagogen** *sew•na•goa•ern*
the temple	**templet** *tehmp•lerdh*
What time is mass/ the service?	**Hvad tid starter messen/ gudstjenesten?** *vadh teedh stah•dah meh•sern/goodhs•tyeh•ner•stern*

Shopping

ESSENTIAL

Where is the market/ mall [shopping centre]?	**Hvor ligger markedet/butikscentret?**	*voar li·gah mah·ker·dherd/boo·teeks·sehn·tahdh*
I'm just looking.	**Jeg ser mig bare omkring.**	*yie sehr mie bah ohm·kring*
Can you help me?	**Kan du hjælpe mig?**	*kan doo yehl·per mie*
I'm being helped.	**Jeg får hjælp.**	*yie faw yehlp*
How much?	**Hvor meget koster det?**	*voar mie·erdh kohs·dah deh*
That's all, thanks.	**Det var det hele, tak.**	*deh vah deh heh·ler tahk*
Where do I pay?	**Hvor kan jeg betale?**	*voar kan yie beh·ta·ler*
I'll pay in cash/by credit card.	**Jeg vil gerne betale kontant/med kreditkort.**	*yie vil gehr·ner beh·ta·ler kohn·tant/mehdh kreh·deet·kawd*
Can I have a receipt?	**Kan jeg få en kvittering?**	*kan yie fow ehn kvee·teh·ring*

At the Shops

Where is...?	**Hvor er...?** *voar ehr...*
the antiques store	**antikvitetshandleren** *an·tee·kvee·tehts·han·lahn*
the bakery	**bageriet** *ba·yah·ree·erdh*
the bank	**banken** *bahnk·ern*
the bookstore	**boghandleren** *bow·han·lahn*

Denmark is an excellent country for shopping. Even in the capital, most shopping can be done on foot. Many of the major international retail stores are located in **Strøget** and **Købmagergade**, Copenhagen´s main pedestrian streets. You can also check out **Vesterbro**, the western part of **Istegade** and the area around **Enghaveplads**. There, you'll find lots of trendy boutiques and pleasant cafes.

For everything under one roof, visit the **Magasin du Nord**, Scandinavia´s largest department store, or the shopping malls: **Field's, Fisketorvet, Frederiksberg Centret** or **Illum.**

Regular store hours are Monday to Friday from 9:00 a.m. to 5:30 p.m. On Friday stores are open until as late as 8:00 p.m. and Saturday they are generally open from 10:00 a.m. to 4:00 or 5:00 p.m. Most stores are closed on Sunday.

the clothing store	**tøjbutikken** <u>toi</u>·boo·tee·gern	
the delicatessen	**delikatesseforretningen** de·li·ka·<u>tehs</u>·ser·foh·reht·ning·ern	
the department store	**stormagasinet** <u>stoar</u>·mah·ga·see·nerdh	
the gift shop	**gavebutikken** <u>ga</u>·ver·boo·tee·gern	
the health food store	**helsekostforretningen** <u>hehl</u>·ser·kohst·foh·reht·ning·ern	
the jeweler	**guldsmeden** <u>gool</u>·smeh·dhern	
Where is…?	**Hvor er…?** Voar ehr…	
the liquor store [off-licence]	**vinhandelen** <u>veen</u>·han·lahn	
the market	**markedet** <u>mah</u>·ker·dherd	
the pastry shop	**konditoriet** kohn·dee·toh·<u>ree</u>·erdh	

the pharmacy [chemist]	**apoteket** *ah·poh·<u>teh</u>·kerdh*
the produce [grocery] store	**købmanden** *<u>kur</u>·man·ern*
the shoe store	**skoforretningen** *<u>skoa</u>·foh·reht·ning·ern*
the shopping mall [centre]	**butikscentret** *boo·<u>teeks</u>·sen·trahdh*
the souvenir store	**souvenirbutikken** *soo·veh·<u>neer</u>·boo·tee·kern*
the supermarket	**supermarkedet** *<u>soo</u>·pah·mah·kerdh*
the tobacconist	**tobakshandlen** *toa·<u>bahks</u>·han·lern*
the toy store	**legetøjsforretningen** *<u>lie</u>·er·tois·foh·reht·ning·ern*

Ask an Assistant

When does...open/ close?	**Hvornår åbner/lukker...?** *voar·naw <u>owb</u>·nah/<u>loa</u>·gah...*
Where is...?	**Hvor er...?** *voar ehr...*
the cashier [cash desk]	**kassen** *<u>ka</u>·sern*
the escalator	**rulletrappen** *<u>roo</u>·ler·trah·bern*
the elevator [lift]	**elevatoren** *eh·ler·va·tohn*
the fitting room	**prøverummene** *<u>prur</u>·ver·roa·mer·ner*
the store directory	**butiksoversigten** *boo·<u>teeks</u>·ow·ah·sig·tern*
Can you help me?	**Kan du hjælpe mig?** *kan doo <u>yehl</u>·per mie*
I'm just looking.	**Jeg ser mig bare omkring.** *yie sehr mie bah ohm·<u>kring</u>*
I'm being helped.	**Jeg får hjælp.** *yie faw yehlp*
Do you have any...?	**Har du nogen...?** *hah doo <u>noa</u>·ern...*
Can you show me...?	**Kan du vise mig...?** *kan doo <u>vee</u>·ser mie...*
Can you ship/wrap it?	**Kan du forsende det/pakke det ind ?** *kan doo foh·<u>seh</u>·ner deh/<u>pah</u>·ger deh in*

| How much? | **Hvor meget koster det?** *voar <u>mie</u>•erdh <u>kohs</u>•dah deh* |
| That's all, thanks. | **Det var det hele, tak.** *deh vah deh <u>heh</u>•ler tahk* |

For Clothing, see page 118.

For Meals & Cooking, see page 64.

For Souvenirs, see page 123.

YOU MAY SEE...

ÅBEN/LUKKET	open/closed
LUKKET FOR FROKOST	closed for lunch
PRØVERUM	fitting room
KASSE	cashier
KUN KONTANTER	cash only
KREDITKORT MODTAGES	credit cards accepted
ÅBNINGSTIDER	business hours
UDGANG	exit

YOU MAY HEAR...

Kan jeg hjælpe dig? *kan yie <u>yehl</u>•per die*	Can I help you?
Lige et øjeblik. *<u>lee</u>•er eht <u>oi</u>•er•blik*	One moment.
Hvad skulle det være? *vadj skoo deh <u>vay</u>•er*	What would you like?
Skulle der være andet? *skoo dehr <u>vay</u>•er <u>a</u>•nerdh*	Anything else?

Personal Preferences

I'd like something...	**Jeg vil gerne have noget...** _yie vil gehr·ner ha noa·erdh..._
cheap/expensive	**billigt/dyrt** _bee·leet/dewrt_
larger/smaller	**mindre/større** _min·drah/stur·ah_
from this region	**fra dette område** _frah deh·ter ohm·row·dher_
Is it real?	**Er det ægte?** _ehr deh ayg·der_
Can you show me this/that?	**Kan du vise mig den her/der?** _kan doo vee·ser mie dehn hehr/dehr_
It's not quite what I want.	**Det er ikke helt det, jeg vil have.** _deh ehr ig·ger hehlt deh yie vil ha_
I don't like it.	**Det bryder jeg mig ikke om.** _deh brew·dhah yie mie ig·ger ohm_
That's too expensive.	**Det er for dyrt.** _deh ehr foh dewrt_
I'd like to think about it.	**Jeg vil gerne tænke lidt over det.** _yie vil gehr·ner tehn·ger lit oh·wah deh_
I'll take it.	**Jeg tager det.** _yie tah deh_

YOU MAY HEAR...

Hvordan ønsker du at betale? _voar·dan urn·skah doo ad beh·ta·ler_	How are you paying?
Dit kreditkort er blevet afvist. _deet kreh·deet·kawd ehr bleh·verdh aw·vihst_	Your credit card has been declined.
ID, tak. _ee deh, tahk_	ID, please.
Vi tager ikke mod kreditkort. _vee ta·er ig·ger modh kreh·deet·kawd_	We don't accept credit cards.
Kun kontant, tak. _koon kohn·tant tahk_	Cash only, please.

Paying & Bargaining

How much?	**Hvor meget koster det?**	voar _mie_•erdh _kohs_•dah deh
I'll pay...	**Jeg vil gerne betale...**	yie vil gehr•ner beh•_ta_•ler
in cash	**kontant**	kohn•_tant_
by credit card	**med kreditkort**	mehdh kreh•_deet_•kawd
by traveler's cheque	**med rejsecheck**	mehdh _rie_•ser•shehk
Can I have a receipt?	**Kan jeg få en kvittering?**	kan yie fow ehn kvee•_teh_•ring
That's too much.	**Det er for meget.**	deh ehr foh _mie_•erdh
I'll give you...	**Jeg kan give dig...**	yie kan gee die...
I only have...kroner.	**Jeg har kun...kroner.**	yie hah koon... _kroa_•nah
Is that your best price?	**Et det den bedste pris, du kan tilbyde mig?**	
		ehr deh dehn _behs_•der pr**ee**s doo kan _til_•bew•dher mie
Can you give me a discount?	**Kan jeg få et nedslag i prisen?**	kan yie fow
		eht _nehdh_•sla ee _pree_•sern

Making a Complaint

I'd like...	**Jeg vil gerne...**	yie vil _gehr_•ner...
to exchange this	**bytte det her**	_bew_•der deh hehr
to return this	**levere det her tilbage**	leh•_veh_•ah deh hehr til•_ba_•yer
a refund	**have mine penge tilbage**	ha _mee_•ner
		pehng•er til•_ba_•yer
to see the manager	**tale med bestyreren**	_ta_•ler mehdh beh•_stew_•ahn

Services

Can you recommend...?	**Kan du anbefale...?**	kan doo _an_•beh•_fa_•ler...
a barber	**en herrefrisør**	ehn _hehr_•er•free•sur
a dry cleaner	**et renseri**	eht rehn•ser•_ree_
a hairstylist	**en frisør**	ehn free•_sur_
a laundromat [launderette]	**et vaskeri**	eht vas•ger•_ree_

a nail salon	**en neglesalon** *ehn nie·ler·sa·long*
a spa	**en spa** *ehn spa*
a travel agency	**et rejsebureau** *eht rie·ser·bew·roa*
Can you...this?	**Kan du...det her?** *kan doo...deh hehr*
alter	**ændre** *ehn·drah*
clean	**rense** *rehn·ser*
mend	**reparere** *reh·pah·reh·ah*
press	**presse** *preh·ser*
When will it be ready?	**Hvornår er det klart?** *voar·naw ehr deh klahd*

Hair & Beauty

I'd like...	**Jeg vil gerne...** *yie vil gehr·ner...*
an appointment for today/tomorrow	**have en tid til i dag/i morgen** *ha ehn teedh til ee da/ee mohn*
some colour/ highlights	**lidt farver/striber** *lit fah·vehr/streeh· bher*
my hair styled/ blow-dried	**have mit hår sat/føntørret** *ha meet haw saht/ streeh· bher*
a haircut	**klippes** *kli·pers*
an eyebrow/bikini wax	**en øjenbrynsvoksning/bikinivoksning** *ehn oi·ern·brewns·vohgs·ning/ bee·kee·nee·vohgs·ning*
a trim	**en studsning** *ehn stuhs·ningh*
a facial	**en ansigtsbehandling** *ehn an·sigts·beh·han·ling*
a manicure/ pedicure	**en manicure/pedicure** *ehn ma·nee·kew·ah/ peh·dee·kew·ah*
a (sports) massage	**en (sports-)massage** *ehn (spohts)ma·sa·sher*
a trim, please...	**en studsning** *ehn stuhs·ningh*
Don't cut it too short.	**Klip det ikke for kort.** *klip deh ig·ger foh koht*
Shorter here.	**Kortere her.** *koh·dah·rah hehr*
Do you offer...?	**Tilbyder I...?** *tiil·bew·dhah ee...*

acupuncture	**akupunktur** *ah·koo·poank·toor*	
aromatherapy	**aromaterapi** *a·roa·ma·teh·rah·pee*	
oxygen treatment	**oxygenbehandling** *ohk·sew·gehn·beh·han·ling*	
Do you have a sauna?	**Har I en sauna?** *hah ee ehn sow·na*	

Many luxury hotels in Denmark offer spa and other health and beauty treatments. Spa resorts and destination spas may be found along the coast throughout Denmark. In recent years the Danish government has instituted rigorous regulations in regard to wellness centers, ensuring a top-quality stay.

Antiques

How old is this?	**Hvor gammelt er det?** *voar gah·merlt ehr deh*
Do you have anything from the…era?	**Har du noget fra…perioden?** *hah doo noa·erdh fra…pehr·ee·oa·dhern*
Will I have problems with customs?	**Får jeg problemer i tolden?** *fow yie proa·bleh·mah ee toh·lern*
Does it come with a certificate of authenticity?	**Følger der et ægthedscertifikat med?** *furl·yah dehr eht ehgt·hehdhs·sehr·tee·fee·kat mehdh*
Can you ship/wrap it?	**Kan I sende/pakke det ind?** *kan ee seh·ner/pah·ker deh in*

Clothing

I'd like…	**Jeg vil gerne have…** *yie vil gehr·ner ha…*
Can I try this on?	**Må jeg prøve det?** *mow yie prur·ver deh*
It doesn't fit.	**Den passer ikke.** *dehn pa·sah ig·ger*
It's too…	**Den er for…** *dehn ehr foh…*
big	**stor** *stoar*
small	**lille** *lee·ler*

short	**kort** *kawd*	
long	**lang** *lahng*	
tight	**tæt** *tayt*	
loose	**løs** *lurs*	
Do you have this in size...?	**Har du den i størrelse...?** *hah doo dehn ee* <u>stur</u>•erl•ser...	
Do you have this in a bigger/smaller size?	**Har du den i en større/mindre størrelse?** *hah doo dehn ee ehn* <u>stur</u>•ah/<u>min</u>•drah <u>stur</u>•erlser	

For Numbers, see page 159.

YOU MAY HEAR...

Du ser godt ud i den. *doo sehr godh oodh ee dehn*	That looks great on you.
Hvordan passer den? *voar•dan pah•ser dehn*	How does it fit?
Vi har ikke din størrelse. *vee hah ig•ger deen stur•rehl•ser*	We don't have your size.

Colors

I'd like something...	**Jeg vil gerne have noget...** *yie vil* <u>gehr</u>•ner ha <u>noa</u>•erdh...	
beige	**beige** *baysh*	
black	**sort** *soart*	
blue	**blåt** *blawht*	
brown	**brunt** *broonht*	

YOU MAY SEE...

HERRETØJ	men's clothing
DAMETØJ	women's clothing
BØRNETØJ	children's clothing

gray	**gråt**	_grawht_
green	**grønt**	_grurnht_
orange	**orange**	_oa·rang·sher_
pink	**lyserødt**	_lew·ser·rurdht_
purple	**violet**	_vee·oa·leht_
red	**rødt**	_rurdht_
white	**hvidt**	_veedht_
yellow	**gult**	_goolt_

Clothes & Accessories

a backpack	**rygsæk**	_rewg·sehk_
a belt	**bælte**	_behl·der_
a bikini	**bikini**	_bee·kee·nee_
a blouse	**bluse**	_bloo·ser_
a bra	**bh**	_beh·how_
underwear	**undertøj**	_oa·nah·tury_
panties	**trusser**	_trush·ser_
a coat	**frakke**	_frah·ger_
a dress	**kjole**	_kyoa·ler_
a hat	**hat**	_hat_
a jacket	**jakke**	_yah·ger_
jeans	**cowboybukser**	_kow·boy·boag·sah_
pajamas	**pyjamas**	_pew·ya·mas_
pants [trousers]	**bukser**	_boag·sah_
panty hose [tights]	**strømpebukser**	_strum·ber·boag·sah_
a purse [handbag]	**håndtaske**	_hawn·tas·ger_
a raincoat	**regnfrakke**	_rien·frah·ger_
a scarf	**tørklæde**	_tur·klay·dher_
a shirt	**skjorte**	_skyoar·der_
shorts	**shorts**	_shohts_
a skirt	**nederdel**	_neh·dhah·dehl_
socks	**sokker**	_soh·gah_

stockings	**strømper** _strum_·bah
a suit	**sæt tøj** m **/dragt** f _seht toi/drahgt_
sunglasses	**solbriller** _soal_·bri·lah
a sweater	**sweater** _sveh_·dah
swimming trunks	**badebukser** _ba_·dher·boag·sah
a swimsuit	**badedragt** _ba_·dher·drahgt
a T-shirt	**t-shirt** _tee_·shurd
a tie	**slips** _slips_
underwear	**underbukser** _oa_·nah·boag·sah

Fabric

I'd like...	**Jeg vil gerne have...** _yie vil gehr·ner ha..._
cotton	**bomuld** _boh_·mool
denim	**denim** _deh_·nim
lace	**blonde** _blohn_·der
leather	**læder** _lay_·dhah
linen	**lærred** _lehr_·erdh
silk	**silke** _sil_·ker
wool	**uld** _ool_

Is it machine washable? **Kan det maskinvaskes?** _kan deh ma·skeen·vas·gers_

Shoes

I'd like...	**Jeg vil gerne have...** _yie vil gehr·ner ha..._
high-heeled/flat shoes	**et par højhælede/flade sko** _eht pah hoi·hay·ler·dher/fla·dher skoa_
boots	**støvler** _sturw_·lah
loafers	**hyttesko** _hew_·der·skoa
sandals	**sandaler** _san·da_·lah
shoes	**sko** _skoa_
slippers	**hjemmesko** _yeh_·mer·skoa
sneakers	**gummisko** _goa_·mee·skoa
In size...	**I størrelse...** _ee stur·erl·ser..._

Sizes

Small (S)	**lille** _lee_·ler
Medium (M)	**medium** _meh_·dee·oam
Large (L)	**stor** stoar
extra large (XL)	**ekstra stor** _ehk_·strah stoar
petite	**petit** peh·_teet_
plus size	**ekstra store størrelser** _ehk_·strah stoa·ah _stur_·erl·sah

Newsagent & Tobacconist

Do you sell English-language books/newspapers?	**Sælger I engelsksprogede bøger/aviser?** _sehl_·yah ee _ehng_·erlsk·spr**ow**·er·dher _bur_·yah/a·_vee_·sah
I'd like...	**Jeg vil gerne have...** yie vil _gehr_·ner ha...
candy [sweets]	**slik** sligh
chewing gum	**tyggegummi** tew·ger·gumh·mee
a chocolate bar	**et stykke chokolade** ehd stewgh·ger sho·ko·ladher
cigars	**nogle cigarer** _noa_·ler see·_gah_·ah
a pack/carton of cigarettes	**en pakke/karton cigaretter** ehn _pah_·ker/kah·_tong_ see·ga·_reh_·dah
a lighter	**en lighter** ehn _lie_·dah
a magazine	**et blad** eht bladh
matches	**nogle tændstikker** _noa_·ler _tehn_·sti·gah
a newspaper	**en avis** ehn a·_vees_
a pen	**en pen** ehn pehn
a postcard	**et postkort** ehd pohst·kawd
a road/town map of...	**et vejkort/bykort over...** eht _vie_·kawd/_bew_·kawd _oh_·wah...
stamps	**nogle frimærker** _noa_·ler _free_·mehr·kah

Photography

I'd like . . . camera.	**Jeg vil gerne have . . . kamera.** *yie vil gehr·ner ha . . . ka·meh·rah*	
an automatic	**et automatisk** *eht ow·toa·ma·tisk*	
a digital	**et digitalt** *eht dee·gee·talt*	
a disposable	**et engangs-** *eht ehn·gahngs-*	
I'd like . . .	**Jeg vil gerne have . . .** *yie vil gehr·ner ha . . .*	
a battery	**et batteri** *eht ba·der·ree*	
digital prints	**nogle digitaltryk** *noa·ler dee·gee·tal·trurk*	
a memory card	**et hukommelseskort** *eht hoo·koh·merl·sers·kawd*	
Can I print digital photos here?	**Kan jeg udprinte digitale billeder her?** *kan yie oodh·prin·der dee·gee·ta·ler bil·ler·dhah hehr*	

Souvenirs

aquavit	**akvavit** *a·kvah·veet*
amber	**rav** *rahw*
antiques	**antikviteter** *an·tee·kvee·teh·dah*
candles	**stearinlys** *steh·reen·lews*
ceramics	**keramik** *keh·rah·meek*
embroidery	**broderi** *broa·dah·ree*
furniture	**møbler** *murb·lah*
glassware	**en glasting** *ehn glas·ting*
handmade crafts	**kunsthåndværk** *koanst·hown·vehrk*
knitwear	**strikvarer** *strik·vah·ah*
hand-printed textiles	**håndtrykte tekstilvarer** *hawn·trurg·der tehk·steel·vah·ah*
May I see this/that ?	**Må jeg se den/det ?** *mow yie seh dehn/deh*
It's the one in the window/display case.	**Det er den i vinduesudstillingen/ montren.** *deh ehr dehn ee vin·doos·oodh· stil·ling·ern/mohn·tren*
I'd like . . .	**Jeg vil gerne have . . .** *yie vil gehr·ner ha . . .*

123

Denmark is known for its modern design and quality craftsmanship around the world. You can peruse the fine silver and jewelry pieces at the **Georg Jensen** shops in Copenhagen and Århus. **Bang & Olufsen**, known internationally for its excellent audiovisual equipment, has shops throughout the country. **Ecco** shoes are easy to find and **Lego** is available in all toy and department stores. **Holmegård Glas, Stelton, Royal Copenhagen** and other well-known Danish designs can be purchased from interior design shops as well as department stores. Though your suitcase might not be big enough, Danes are also famous for their sleek and practical modern furniture.

a battery	**et batteri**	eht ba·der·<u>ree</u>
a bracelet	**et armbånd**	eht <u>ahm</u>·bawn
a brooch	**en broche**	ehn <u>broh</u>·sher
earrings	**et par ørenringe**	eht pah <u>ur</u>·ahn·ring·er
a necklace	**en halskæde**	ehn hals·<u>kay</u>·dher
a ring	**en ring**	ehn ring
a watch	**et ur**	eht oor
I'd like...	**Jeg vil gerne have...**	yie vil <u>gehr</u>·ner ha...
copper	**kobber**	<u>koh</u>·wah
crystal	**krystal**	krew·<u>stal</u>
diamonds	**diamanter**	dee·a·<u>mand</u>
white/yellow gold	**hvidguld/rødguld**	<u>veedh</u>·gool/<u>rurdh</u>·gool
pearls	**perler**	<u>pehr</u>·lah
pewter	**tinlegering**	tin·leh·<u>sheh</u>·ring
platinum	**platin**	pla·<u>teen</u>
sterling silver	**sterlingsølv**	<u>stehr</u>·ling·surl
Is this real?	**Er det ægte?**	ehr deh <u>ehg</u>·ter
Can you engrave it?	**Kan du indgravere det?**	kan doo <u>in</u>·grah·veh·er deh

ESSENTIAL

When's the game?	**Hvornår starter kampen?**
	voar•naw stah•dah kahm•bern
Where's...?	**Hvor er...?** *voar ehr...*
the beach	**stranden** *strah•nern*
the park	**parken** *pah•gern*
the pool	**svømmebassinet** *svur•mer•ba•sehng•erdh*
Is it safe to swim/	**Er det sikkert at svømme/dykke her?** *ehr*
dive here?	*deh sig•gahd ad svur•mer/dur•ker hehr*
Can I hire golf	**Kan jeg leje golfkøller?** *kan yie lie•er*
clubs?	*gohlf•kur•lah*
How much per hour?	**Hvad koster det per time?** *vadh kohs•dah*
	deh pehr tee•mer
How far is it to...?	**Hvor langt er der til...?** *voar lahngt ehr dehr til...*
Can you show me on	**Kan du vise mig det på kortet?** *kan doo*
the map?	*vee•ser mie deh paw kaw•derdh*

Watching Sport

When's...?	**Hvornår starter...?** *voar•naw stah•dah...*
the baseball game	**baseballkampen** *baseball•kahm•pern*
the basketball game	**basketballkampen** *bah•skerd•bowl•kahm•bern*
the boxing match	**boksekampen** *bohk•ser•kahm•bern*
the cricket game	**cricketkampen** *cricket• kahm•pern*
the cycling race	**cykelløbet** *sew•kerl•lur•berdh*
the golf	**golfturneringen** *gohlf•toor•neh•ing•ern*
tournament	
the soccer [football]	**fodboldkampen** *foadh•bohld•kahm•bern*
game	

the tennis match	**tenniskampen**	_teh_·nees·kahm·bern
the volleyball game	**volleyballkampen**	_voh_·lee·bawl·kahm·bern
Who's playing?	**Hvem spiller?**	vehm speel·lah
Where's...?	**Hvor er...?**	voar ehr...
the horsetrack	**hestevæddeløbsbanen**	
		hehs·der·**vay**·dher·lurbs·ba·nern
the racetrack	**væddeløbsbanen**	_vay_·dher·lurbs·ba·nern
the stadium	**stadiumet**	_sta_·dee·oa·merdh
Where can I place a bet?	**Hvor kan jeg vædde?**	voar kan yie _**vay**_·dher

Playing Sport

Where's...?	**Hvor er...?**	voar ehr...
the golf course	**golfbanen**	_gohlf_·ba·nern
the gym	**motionscentret**	moa·_shoans_·cehn·tahdh
the park	**parken**	_pah_·gern
the tennis courts	**tennisbanerne**	ten·nis·ba·nah·ner
How much per...?	**Hvad koster det per...?**	vadh kohs·dah deh pehr...
day	**dag**	da

Danes are very active people and most of the population participates in regular sporting activities. Sports can mean two things for Danes: **idræt** (an old Scandinavian word for sports) and **sport** (the contemporary term). **Idræt** often refers to the ideas of team-building and well-being associated with playing sports, while **sport** is related to the ideas of performance and athletic achievement.

If you are looking for an active vacation, you can find lots of opportunities for engaging in activities like cycling, sailing, soccer, handball, badminton, horseback riding, fishing and swimming, which are all popular. If you prefer to sit back and watch, sports are regularly broadcast on TV and there are many live events.

hour	**time** *tee·mer*	
game	**spil** *spil*	
round	**runde** *roan·der*	
Can I hire…?	**Kan jeg leje…?** *kan yie lie·er…*	
golf clubs	**golfkøller** *gohlf·kur·lah*	
equipment	**udstyr** *oodh·stewr*	
a racket	**en ketcher** *ehn keht·shah*	

At the Beach/Pool

Where's the beach/pool?	**Hvor ligger stranden/poolen?** *voar li·gah strah·nern/poo·lern*	
Is there…?	**Er der…?** *ehr dehr…*	
a kiddie [paddling] pool	**et børnebassin** *eht bur·ner·ba·sehng*	
an indoor/outdoor pool	**en indendørs/udendørs pool** *ehn in·ern·durs/oo·dhern·durs pool*	
a lifeguard	**en livredder** *ehn leew·ray·dhah*	
Is it safe…?	**Er det sikkert…?** *ehr deh si·gaht…*	
to swim	**at gå i vandet her** *ad gow ee van·erdh hehr*	
to dive	**at dykke her** *ad dur·ker hehr*	
for children	**for børnene** *foh bur·ner·ner*	
I want to hire…	**Jeg vil gerne leje…** *yie vil gehr·ner lie·er…*	
a deck chair	**en liggestol** *ehn lig·ger·stoal*	
diving equipment	**noget dykkerudstyr** *eht dur·gah·oodh·stewr*	
a jet-ski	**nogle jetski** *noa·ler jeht·skee*	

Danes are fans of beach vacations and water sports. There are more than 270 marinas around the country and all different types of boats and other equipment can be rented. If you rent a jet-ski or windsurfer, keep in mind that, in an effort to protect the wildlife, Denmark has very strict rules regarding where they may be used.

a motorboat	**en motorbåd** *ehn moa·tah·bowdh*
a rowboat	**en robåd** *ehn roa·bawdh*
snorkling equipment	**noget snorkleudstyr** *noa·erdh snoh·kler·oodh·stewr*
a surfboard	**et surfbræt** *eht surf breht*
a towel	**et håndklæde** *eht hawn·klay·dher*
an umbrella	**en parasol** *ehn pah·rah·sohl*
water-skis	**et par vandski** *eht pah van·skee*
a windsurfer	**en windsurfer** *ehn win·sur·fer*
For…hours.	**I…timer.** *ee…tee·mah*

For Traveling with Children, see page 138.

The mild climate and topography of Denmark are not particularly good for winter sports. However, ice hockey and ice skating are popular.

Winter Sports

A lift pass for a day/ five days, please.	**Et liftkort til en dag/fem dage.** *ehd lift·kawd til ehn da/fehm dae*
Where's the ice rink?	**Hvor er skøjtebanen.** *voar ehr skoi·der·ba·nern*
Are there lessons?	**Tilbyder I undervisning?** *til·bew·dhah ee oa·nah·vees·ning*
How much?	**Hvor meget koster det?** *voar mie·erdh kohs·dah deh*
I'm a beginner.	**Jeg er begynder.** *yie her beh·guw·nah*
I'm experienced.	**Jeg har erfaring.** *yie hah ehr·fahring*
I'd like to rent ice skates.	**Jeg vil gerne leje et par skøjter.** *yie vil gehr·ner lie·er eht pah skoi·dah*
I'd like to hire…	**Jeg vil gerne leje …** *yie vil gehr·ner lie·yer*
boots	**støvler** *sturvl·lah*
a helmet	**en hjelm** *ehn yelm*
poles	**stave** *stah·ve*

skis	**ski** *skih*
a snowboard	**et snowboard** *ehd snowboard*
snowshoes	**snesko** *sneh·skoa*
These are too big/ small.	**De er for store/små.** *dee ehr foh stoa·ah/smow*
A trail map, please.	**Et løjpekort.** *ehd lury·peh·kowd*

Out in the Country

I'd like a map of...	**Jeg vil gerne have et kort over...** *yie vil gehr·ner ha eht kawd ow·ah...*
this region	**dette område** *deh·deh ohm·row·dher*
walking routes	**vandreruter** *vahn·drah·roo·dah*
bike routes	**cykelruter** *sew·kerl·roo·dah*
the trails	**gangstier** *gahng·stee·ah*
Is it easy/difficult?	**Er det nemt/svært?** *ehr deh nehmt/svehrt*
Is it far/steep?	**Er det langt herfra/stejlt?** *ehr deh lahngt hehr·frah/stielt*
How far is it to...?	**Hvor langt er der til...?** *voar lahngt ehr dehr til...*
Can you show me on the map?	**Kan du vise mig det på kortet?** *kan doo vee·ser mie deh paw kaw·derdh*
I'm lost.	**Jeg er faret vild.** *yie ehr fah·erdh veel*
Where's...?	**Hvor er...?** *voar ehr...*
the bridge	**broen** *broa·ern*
the cave	**hulen** *hoo·lern*
the cliff	**klippen** *kli·bern*
the farm	**bondegården** *boa·ner·gaw·ern*
the field	**marken** *mah·gern*
the forest	**skoven** *skow·ern*
the hill	**bakken** *bah·gern*
the lake	**søen** *sur·ern*
the nature preserve	**naturreservatet** *na·toor·reh·sah·va·derdh*
the viewpoint	**udkigsposten** *oodh·keegs·pohs·dern*
the park	**parken** *pah·gern*

the path	**stien** <u>stee</u>•ern
the peak	**toppen** toph•ern
the picnic area	**picnicområdet** <u>pik</u>•nik•ohm•**row**•dherd
the pond	**dammen** <u>dahm</u>•mern
the river	**floden** <u>floa</u>•dhern
the sea	**havet** <u>ha</u>•verdh
the hot spring	**den varme kilde** dehn vah•mern kilh•er
the stream	**åen** <u>ow</u>•ern
the valley	**dalen** da•lern
the vineyard	**vingården** veen•gaw•ern
the waterfall	**vandfaldet** van•falh•ehd

Going Out

ESSENTIAL

What is there to do in the evenings?	**Hvad laver man her om aftenen?** Vadh <u>la</u>•vah man hehr ohm <u>af</u>•tern
Do you have a program of events?	**Har du et program over arrangementerne?** hah doo eht proa•grahm <u>ow</u>•ah ah•rahng•sheh•<u>mang</u>•ah•ner
What's playing at the movies [cinema] tonight?	**Hvad går der i biografen i aften?** vadh gaw dehr ee bee•oa•<u>gra</u>•fern ee <u>af</u>•tern
Where's...?	**Hvor er...?** voar ehr...
the downtown area	**den indre by** dehn <u>in</u>•drah bew
the bar	**baren** <u>bah</u>•ern
the dance club	**diskoteket** dees•koa•<u>teh</u>•kerd
Is there a cover charge?	**Koster det noget at komme ind?** <u>kohs</u>•dah deh <u>noa</u>•erdh ad <u>koh</u>•mer in

Culturally, there is a lot to enjoy in Denmark. Ballet has been a tradition since the 17th century. The Royal Theater produces plays in a range of genres by both Danish and foreign playwrights. Danish film is also internationally known and has been dominated in recent years by Lars Von Trier.

If you are interested in the visual arts, visit the **Louisiana museum.** Located on the North Zealand coast, it is accessible by car or train. The museum houses an important collection of modern and contemporary art and is located on spectacular seaside property.

Entertainment

Can you recommend…?	**Kan du anbefale…?** kan doo <u>an</u>•beh•**fa**•ler…
a concert	**en koncert** ehn kohn•<u>sehrt</u>
a movie	**en film** ehn film
an opera	**en opera** ehn <u>oa</u>•peh•rah
a play	**et teaterstykke** eht teh•**a**•dah•stur•ger
When does it start/ end ?	**Hvad tid starter/slutter det?** vadh teedh <u>stah</u>•dah/<u>sloo</u>•dah deh
What's the dress code?	**Er der nogen regler for påklædning?** ehr dehr <u>noa</u>•ern <u>ray</u>•lah foh <u>pow</u>•klaydh•ning
I like…	**Jeg kan godt lide…** yie kan gohd lee…
classical music	**klassisk musik** <u>kla</u>•seesk moo•<u>seek</u>

YOU MAY HEAR…

Sluk venligst din mobiltelefon.
sloak <u>vehn</u>•leest deen moa•<u>beel</u>•teh•ler•foan

Turn off your cell [mobile] phones.

folk music	**folkemusik** _fohl_·ker·moo·seek
jazz	**jazz** djas
pop music	**popmusik** _pohp_·moo·seek
rap	**rapmusik** _rahp_·moo·seek

For Tickets, see page 20.

> There are countless festivals scheduled throughout the year in Denmark. Tourist information offices, travel agencies, hotels and guide books offer extensive information about local as well as national celebrations. A handful of the annual events include the Copenhagen Marathon, Green Mermaid Festival, Beer Festival, Copenhagen Jazz Festival and Roskilde Festival of rock music. Also, if you're near the coast in June, Midsummer Night, the longest night of the year, is a fun event, traditionally celebrated with bonfires and other festivities.

Nightlife

What is there to do in the evenings?	**Hvad laver man her om aftenen?** _Vadh la·vah man hehr ohm af·tern_
Can you recommend...?	**Kan du anbefale...?** _kan doo an·beh·fa·ler..._
a bar	**en bar** _ehn bah_
a casino	**et kasino** _eht ka·see·noa_
a dance club	**et diskotek** _eht dee·skoa·tehk_
a gay club	**et bøssediskotek** _eht bur·ser·dee·skoa·tehk_
a jazz club	**en jazzklub** _ehn jazz·kluhb_
a club with Danish music	**et spillested med dansk musik** _ehd spee·ler·stedh medh dansk muh·sikh_
a nightclub	**en natklub** _ehn nat·kloob_

A favorite Danish pastime is visiting pubs, though you can also find wine bars and cocktail bars. A traditional pub is called a **bodega** (beer bar). There you'll see Danes enjoying the local brews and playing dice. Dice can be requested at the bar.

Another option is to check out the many **hyggelige** cafes. Cafes range from those where you can order a drink and a simple sandwich to those with sophisticated decor and jet-set clientele.

If you're in the mood for music, there are plenty of dance clubs as well as regular live music shows to be found.

Is there live music?	**Er der live musik?** *ehr dehr liev moo•seek*
How do I get there?	**Hvordan kommer jeg derhen?** *voar•dan koh•mah yie dehr•hehn*
Is there a cover charge?	**Koster det noget at komme ind?** *kohs•dah det noa•erdh ad koh•mer in*
Let's go dancing.	**Lad og gå ud og danse.** *ladh ohs gow oodh ow dan•ser*
Is this area safe at night?	**Er dette område sikkert om natten?** *ehr deh•ter ohm•row•dhe sig•gard ohm na•dern*

Special Requirements

Business Travel

ESSENTIAL

I'm here on business.	**Jeg er her på forretningsrejse.** yie ehr hehr paw foh·_reht_·nings·rie·ser
Here's my business card.	**Her er mit visitkort.** hehr ehr meet vee·_seet_·kawd
Can I have your card?	**Må jeg få dit visitkort?** mow yie fow deet vee·_seet_·kawd
I have a meeting with…	**Jeg har et møde med…** yie hah eht _mur_·dher mehdh…
Where's…?	**Hvor er…?** voar ehr…
the business center	**businesscentret** _bis_·nis·sehn·tahdh
the convention hall	**konferencesalen** kohn·fer·_rahng_·ser·sa·lern
the meeting room	**mødelokalet** _mur_·dher·loa·ka·lerdh

135

On Business

I'm here to attend…	**Jeg er her for at deltage i et…** yie ehr hehr foh ad _dehl_·ta·yer ee eht…
a seminar	**et seminar** eht seh·mee·_nah_
a conference	**en konference** ehn kohn·fer·_rahng_·ser
a meeting	**et møde** eht _mur_·dher
My name is…	**Mit navn er…** meet nown ehr…
May I introduce my colleague…	**Må jeg præsentere dig for min kollega…** mow yie pray·sehn·_teh_·ah die foh meen koa·_leh_·ga…
I have a meeting/an appointment with…	**Jeg har et møde/en aftale med…** yie hah eht _mur_·dher/ehn _ow_·ta·ler mehdh…
I'm sorry I'm late.	**Jeg beklager, at jeg kommer for sent.** yie beh·_kla_·yah ad yie _koh_·mah foh sehnt

I need an interpreter.	**Jeg har brug for en tolk.** *yie hah broo foh ehn tohlk*
You can reach me at the…Hotel.	**Du kan træffe mig på Hotel…** *doo kan treh·fer mie paw hoa·tehl…*
I'm here until…	**Jeg er her indtil den…** *yie ehr hehr in·til dehn…*
I need to…	**Jeg har brug for at…** *yie hah broo foh ad…*
make a call	**lave en opringning** *la·ver ehn ohb·ring·ning*
make a photocopy	**tage en fotokopi** *ta·er ehn foa·toa·koa·pee*
send an e-mail	**sende en e-mail** *sehn·ner ehn e·mail*
send a fax	**sende en fax** *sehn·ner ehn fahks*
send a package (overnight)	**sende en pakke (ekspres)** *sehn·ner ehn pah·ger (ehks·prehs)*
It was a pleasure to meet you.	**Det glæder mig at træffe dig.** *deh glay·dhah mie ad treh·fer die*

For Communications, see page 48.

YOU MAY HEAR...

Har du en aftale? *hah doo ehn <u>ow</u>•ta•ler* Do you have an appointment?

Med hvem? *mehdh vehm* With whom?

Han/Hun sidder i møde. *han/hoon <u>si</u>•dhah ee <u>mur</u>•dher* He/She is in a meeting.

Lige et øjeblik. *<u>lee</u>•er eht <u>oi</u>•er•blik* One moment, please.

Sid ned. *sidh nehdh* Have a seat.

Vil du have noget at drikke? *vil doo hah noa•erdh ad drihg•ger* Would you like something to drink?

Tak fordi du kom. *tahk foh•<u>dee</u> doo kohm* Thank you for coming.

Danes tend to get right to business and don't engage in much small talk. When asked to give a briefing, be detailed, since Danes are rather meticulous. You'll find Danes to be comparatively serious and direct in business dealings and in their manner of speaking in general. This is not meant to insult. Though they are relatively informal, avoid comments that might be taken as personal.

Traveling with Children

ESSENTIAL

Is there a discount for kids?	**Er det billigere for børn?** *ehr deh <u>bee</u>·lee·ah foh burn*
Can you recommend a babysitter?	**Kan du anbefale en babysitter?** *kan doo <u>an</u>·beh·<u>fa</u>·ler ehn <u>bay</u>·bee·si·dah?*
Can we have a child's seat/ highchair ?	**Må vi få et barnesæde/en høj stol?** *mow vee fow eht <u>bah</u>·ner·<u>say</u>·dher/ehn hoi st<u>oal</u>*
Where can I change the baby?	**Hvor kan jeg skifte babyen?** *voar kan yie <u>skeef</u>·der <u>bay</u>·bee·ern*

Out & About

Can you recommend something for the kids?	**Kan du anbefale noget til børnene?** *kan doo <u>an</u>·beh·<u>fa</u>·ler <u>noa</u>·erdh til <u>bur</u>·ner·ner*
Where's...?	**Hvor er...?** *voar ehr...*
the amusement park	**forlystelsesparken** *foh·<u>lur</u>·stehl·sers·<u>pah</u>·kern*
the arcade	**spillehallen** *<u>spih</u>·ler·hal·lern*
the kiddie [paddling] pool	**børnebassinet** *<u>bur</u>·ner·ba·sehng·erdh*
the park	**parken** <u>pah</u>·gern
the playground	**legepladsen** *<u>lie</u>·er·pla·sern*
the zoo	**den zoologiske have** *dehn soa·<u>loa</u>·gee·sker <u>ha</u>·ver*

Are kids allowed?	**Er der adgang for børn?** *ehr dehr <u>adh</u>•gahng foh burn*
Is it safe for kids?	**Er det sikkert for børnene?** *ehr deh <u>si</u>•gaht foh <u>bur</u>•ner•ner*
Is it suitable for… year olds?	**Egner det sig til…årige?** <u>ie</u>•nah deh sie til… <u>aw</u>•ree•yer

For Numbers, see page 159.

YOU MAY HEAR…

Hvor er han/hun sød! *voar ehr han/ hoon surdh*	How cute he/she is!
Hvad hedder han/hun? *vadh <u>heh</u>• dhah han/hoon*	What's his/her name?
Hvor gammel er han/hun? *voar <u>gah</u>• merl her han/hoon*	How old is he/she?

Baby Essentials

Do you have…?	**Har du…?** *har doo…*
a baby bottle	**en suttefl aske** *ehn soo•der•flas•ker*
baby food	**babymad** *bay•bew•madh*
baby wipes	**nogen vådservietter** *noa•ern voadh•sehr•vee•eh•dah*
a car seat	**et barnesæde** *eht bah•ner•say•dher*
a children's menu	**en børnemenu** *ehn bur•ner•meh•new*
a children's portion	**en børneportioner** *bur•ner•poh•shoa•nah*
a child's seat/ highchair	**et barnesæde/en høj stol** *eht bah•ner•say•dher/ehn hoi stoal*
a crib	**en barneseng** *ehn bah•ner•sehng*
diapers [nappies]	**nogen bleer** *noa•ern bleh•ah*
formula	**noget mælkeerstatning** *noa•erdh mehl•ker•ehr•stad•ning*
a pacifier [dummy]	**en sut** *ehn soot*
a playpen	**en kravlegård** *ehn krow•ler•gaw*
a stroller [pushchair]	**en klapvogn** *ehn klahp•vown*
Can I breastfeed the baby here?	**Må jeg amme babyen her?** *mow yie ah•mer bay•bee•ern hehr*

| Where can I change the baby? | **Hvor kan jeg skifte babyen?** *voar kan yie <u>skeef</u>·der <u>bay</u>·bee·ern* |

For Dining with Children, see page 62.

Babysitting

Can you recommend a reliable babysitter?	**Kan du anbefale en pålidelig babysitter?** *kan doo <u>an</u>·beh·<u>fa</u>·ler ehn paw·<u>lee</u>·dher·lee <u>bay</u>·bee·si·dah*
What's the charge?	**Hvad koster det?** *vadh <u>kohs</u>·dah deh*
We'll be back by...	**Vi er tilbage klokken...** *vee ehr til·<u>ba</u>·yer <u>kloh</u>·gern...*
I can be reached at...	**Jeg kan træffes på...** *yie kan <u>treh</u>·fers pow...*

For Time, see page 161.

Health & Emergency

Can you recommend a pediatrician?	**Kan du anbefale en børnelæge?** *kan doo <u>an</u>·beh·<u>fa</u>·ler ehn <u>bur</u>·ner·<u>lay</u>·er*
My child is allergic to...	**Mit barn er allergisk overfor...** *meet b**ah**n ehr a·<u>lehr</u>·gisk <u>ow</u>·ah·foh...*
My child is missing.	**Mit barn er blevet væk.** *meet b**ah**n ehr <u>bleh</u>·werdh vehk*
Have you seen a boy/girl?	**Har du set en dreng/pige?** *hah doo seht ehn drehng/<u>pee</u>·er*

For Meals & Cooking, see page 64.

For Health, see page 147.

For Police, see page 146.

Disabled Travelers

ESSENTIAL

Is there…?	**Er der…?** *ehr dehr…*
access for the disabled	**adgang for handicappede** <u>*adh*</u>*·gahng for* <u>*han*</u>*·dee·kahp·per·dher*
a wheelchair ramp	**en rampe til kørestole** *ehn* <u>*rahm*</u>*·ber til* <u>*kur*</u>*·ah·stoa·ler*
a disabled-accessible toilet	**et handicaptoilet** *eht* <u>*han*</u>*·dee·kahp·toa·ee·lehd*
I need…	**Jeg har brug for…** *yie hah broo foh…*
assistance	**hjælp** *yehlp*
an elevator [lift]	**en elevator** *ehn eh·ler·*<u>*va*</u>*·toh*
a ground-floor room	**et værelse i stueetagen** *eht* <u>*vehrl*</u>*·ser ee* <u>*stoo*</u>*·er·eh·ta·shern*

Asking for Assistance

I'm disabled.

Jeg er handicappet.
yie ehr<u>han</u>·dee·kah·perdh

I'm deaf.

Jeg er døv. *yie ehr durv*

I'm visually/hearing impaired.

Jeg er synshæmmet/hørehæmmet . *yie ehr <u>sewns</u>·heh·merdh/<u>hur</u>·ah·hehm·merdh*

I'm unable to walk far/use the stairs.

Jeg kan ikke gå langt/op ad trapperne. *yie kan <u>ig</u>·ger gow lahngt/ohb a <u>trah</u>·bah·ner*

Can I bring my wheelchair?

Må jeg tage min kørestol med? *mow yie ta meen <u>kur</u>·ah·st<u>oa</u>l mehdh*

Are guide dogs permitted?

Er der adgang for førerhunde? *ehr dehr <u>adh</u>·gahng foh <u>fur</u>·ah·hoo·ner*

Can you help me?

Kan du hjælpe mig? *kan doo <u>yehl</u>·per mie*

Please open/hold the door.

Åbn/Hold venligst døren. *owbn/hohl <u>vehn</u>·leest <u>dur</u>·ern*

In an Emergency

Emergencies

ESSENTIAL

Help!	**Hjælp!** *yehlp*
Go away!	**Gå væk!** *gow vehk*
Stop thief!	**Stop tyven!** *stohp tew•vern*
Get a doctor!	**Tilkald læge!** *til•kal lay•er*
Fire!	**Det brænder!** *deh brahn•nah*
I'm lost.	**Jeg er faret vild** *yie ehr fah•erdh veel*
Can you help me?	**Kan du hjælpe mig?** *kan doo yehl•per mie*

145

YOU MAY HEAR...

Udfyld venligst denne formular. *oodh•fewl vehn•leest deh•neh foh•moo•lah* — Fill out this form.

Vis venligst dit ID. *Vees vehn•leesd deet ee deh* — Your ID, please.

Hvornår/Hvor skete det? *voar•naw/voar skeh•der deh* — When/Where did it happen?

Hvordan ser han/hun ud? *voar•dan sehr han hoon oodh* — What does he/she look like?

Police

ESSENTIAL

Call the police!	**Ring til politiet!** *ring til poa·lee·**tee**·erdh*
Where's the police station?	**Hvor ligger politistationen?** *voar <u>li</u>·gah poa·lee·**tee**·sta·sh**oa**·nern*
There has been an accident/attack.	**Der er sket en ulykke/et overfald.** *dehr ehr skeht ehn <u>oo</u>·lur·ker/eht <u>ow</u>·ah·fal*
My child is missing.	**Mit barn er blevet væk.** *meet bahn ehr <u>bleh</u>·erdh vehk*
I need...	**Jeg har brug for...** *yie hah br**oo** foh...*
an interpreter	**en tolk** *ehn tohlk*
to contact my lawyer	**at tale med min advokat** *ad <u>ta</u>·ler mehdh meen adh·voa·<u>kat</u>*
to make a phone call	**at lave en opringning** *ad <u>la</u>·ver ehn <u>ohb</u>·ring·ning*
I'm innocent.	**Jeg er uskyldig.** *yie ehr oo·<u>skewl</u>·dee*

Crime & Lost Property

I want to report...	**Jeg vil anmelde...** *yie vil <u>an</u>·meh·ler...*
a mugging	**et overfald** *eht <u>ow</u>·ah·fal*
a rape	**en voldtægt** *ehn <u>vohl</u>·tehkt*
a theft	**et tyveri** *eht tew·ah·<u>ree</u>*
I've been robbed/ mugged	**Jeg er blevet bestjålet/overfaldet.** *yie ehr <u>bleh</u>·erdh beh·st**yow**·lerdh/<u>ow</u>·ah·fa·lerdh*
I've lost...	**Jeg har tabt...** *yie hah tahbt...*
...has been stolen.	**... er blevet stjålet.** *...ehr <u>bleh</u>·erdh st**yow**·lerdh*
My backpack	**Min rygsæk** *meen <u>rewg</u>·sehk*
My bicycle	**Min cykel** *meen <u>sew</u>·gel*

My camera	**Mit kamera** meet _ka_·meh·rah
My (rental) car	**Min (lejede) bil** meen (_lie_·er·dher) beel
My computer	**Min pc** meen peh·_seh_
My credit cards	**Mit kreditkort** meet kreh·_deet_·kawd
My jewelry	**Mine smykker** _mee_·ner _smur_·kah
My money	**Mine penge** _mee_·ner _pehng_·er
My passport	**Mit pas** meet pas
My purse [handbag]	**Min håndtaske** meen _hawn_·tas·ger
...has been stolen.	**...er blevet stjålet.** ...ehr _bleh_·erdh _styow_·lerdh
My traveler's cheques	**Mine rejsechecks** _mee_·ner _rie_·ser·shehk
My wallet	**Min tegnebog** meen _tie_·ner·bow
I need a police report for my insurance.	**Jeg skal bruge en politianmeldelse til min forsikring.** yie skal _broo_·er ehn poa·lee·_tee_·an·meh·lerl·ser til meen foh·_sik_·ring
Where is the British/American/Irish embassy?	**Hvor er den den engelske/amerikanske/irske ambassade?** Voar ehr dehn _en_·ghel·sger/ _ama_·ree·kansger/ir·sger _amh_·bah·sa·dher

147

Health

ESSENTIAL

I'm sick [ill].	**Jeg er syg.** yie ehr sew
I need an English-speaking doctor.	**Jeg har brug for en læge, der taler engelsk.** yie hah broo foh ehn _lay_·er dehr _ta_·lah ehng·erlsk
It hurts here.	**Det gør ondt her.** deh gur ohnt hehr
I have a stomachache.	**Jeg har mavepine.** yie hah _ma_·ver·_pee_·ner

Finding a Doctor

Can you recommend a doctor/dentist?	**Kan du anbefale en læge/tandlæge?** *kan doo <u>an</u>•beh•<u>fa</u>•ler ehn <u>lay</u>•er/<u>tan</u>•<u>lay</u>•er*
Can the doctor come to see me here?	**Kunne lægen komme for at se mig her?** *<u>koo</u>•ner <u>lay</u>•ern <u>koh</u>•mer foh ad seh mie hehr*
I need an English-speaking doctor.	**Jeg har brug for en læge, der taler engelsk.** *yie hah br<u>oo</u> foh ehn <u>lay</u>•er dehr <u>ta</u>•lah <u>ehng</u>•erlsk*
What are the office hours?	**Hvornår er der åbent?** *voar•<u>naw</u> ehr dehr <u>ow</u>•bernt*
Can I make an appointment...?	**Kan jeg få en tid...?** *kan yie fow ehn teedh...*
for today	**i dag** *ee da*
for tomorrow	**i morgen** *ee m<u>oh</u>n*
as soon as possible	**så snart som muligt** *saw snaht sohm <u>moo</u>•leet*
It's urgent.	**Det haster.** *deh <u>has</u>•dah*

Symptoms

I'm...	**Jeg...** *yie...*
bleeding	**bløder** *<u>blur</u>•dhah*
constipated	**er forstoppet** *ehr foh•<u>stoh</u>•berdh*
dizzy	**er svimmel** *ehr <u>svim</u>•merl*
nauseous	**har kvalme** *hah <u>kval</u>•mer*
vomiting	**har kastet op** *hah <u>kas</u>•derdh ohb*
It hurts here.	**Det gør ondt her.** *deh gur ohnt hehr*
I have...	**Jeg har...** *yie hah...*
an allergic reaction	**en allergisk reaktion** *ehn a•<u>lehr</u>•geesk reh•ahk•<u>shoan</u>*
chest pain	**brystsmerter** *<u>brurst</u>•smehr•dah*
cramps	**kramper** *krahm•bar*
diarrhea	**diarré** *dia•rah*
an earache	**ondt i ørerne** *ohnt ee <u>ur</u>•ah•ner*
a fever	**feber** *<u>feh</u>•bah*

pain	**smerter** _smehr_•dah
a rash	**fået udslet** _fow_•erdh _oodh_•sleht
a sprain	**en forstuvning** ehn for•stuw•ning
some swelling	**fået en hævelse** _fow_•erdh ehn _hay_•vel•ser
a stomachache	**mavepine** _ma_•ver•pee•ner
sunstroke	**solstik** _soal_•stik
I've been sick for...days.	**Jeg har været syg i...dage.** yie hah _vay_•erdh sew ee... _da_•er

For Numbers, see page159.

Conditions

I'm...	**Jeg har...** yie hah...
anemic	**blodmangel** _bloadh_•mahng•erl
asthmatic	**astma** _ast_•ma
diabetic	**sukkersyge** _soa_•gah•sew•er
I'm epileptic	**Jeg er epileptiker** yie ehr epi•lehp•tiger
I'm allergic to antibiotics/penicillin.	**Jeg er allergisk over for antibiotika/ pencilin.** yie ehr a•_lehr_•geesk _ow_•ah•foh an•tee•bee•_oa_•tee•ka/pehn•see•_leen_
I have arthritis/(high/ low) blood pressure	**Jeg har gigt/(højt/lavt) blodtryk.** yie hah geegt/(hoit/lavt) _bloadh_•truk
I'm on...	**Jeg tager...** yie tah...

| I have a heart condition. | **Jeg har en hjertesygdom.** *yie hah ehn* *<u>yehr</u>•der•**sew**•dohm* |

For Meals & Cooking, see page 64.

Treatment

Do I need a prescription/ medicine?	**Skal jeg have en recept/medicin?** *skal yie hah ehn reh•cebt/meh•di•cin*
Can you prescribe a generic drug [unbranded medication]?	**Kan du udskrive den billigste medicin?** *kan doo oodh•skriwe dehn bee•lees •der* *meh•di•cin*
Where can I get it?	**Hvor kan jeg få det?** *voar kan yie fow deh*

For Pharmacy, see page 152.

YOU MAY HEAR...

Hvad er der galt? *vadh ehr dehr galt*	What's wrong?
Hvor gør det ondt? *voar gur deh ohnt*	Where does it hurt?
Gør det ondt her? *gur deh ohnt hehr*	Does it hurt here?
Tager du nogen anden medicin? *tah doo* *<u>noa</u>•ern <u>a</u>•nern meh•dee•<u>seen</u>*	Are you taking any other on medication?
Er du allergisk over for noget? *ehr doo* *a•<u>lehr</u>•geesk <u>ow</u>•ah•foh <u>noa</u>•erdh*	Are you allergic to anything?
Luk munden op. *loak <u>moa</u>•nern ohb*	Open your mouth.
Tag en dyb indånding. *ta ehn dewb* *in•own•ning*	Breathe deeply.
Vær venlig at hoste. *vehr <u>vehn</u>•lee ad <u>hohs</u>•der*	Cough, please.
Du skal indlægges på hospitalet til **undersøgelse.** *doo skal <u>in</u>•lay•gers paw* *hoa•spee•<u>ta</u>•lerdh til <u>oa</u>•nah•<u>sur</u>•yerl•ser*	I want you to go to the hospital.

Hospital

Please notify my family.	**Vær venlig og underret min familie.** *vehr vehn·lee ow oa·nah·reht meen fa·meel·yer*
I'm in pain.	**Jeg har smerter.** *yie hah smehr·dah*
I need a doctor/nurse.	**Jeg har brug for en læge/sygeplejerske.** *yie hah broo foh ehn lay·er/sew·er·plie·ah·sker*
When are visiting hours?	**Hvornår er der besøgstid?** *voar·naw ehr dehr beh·surs·teedh*
I'm visiting...	**Jeg er her for at besøge...** *yie ehr hehr foh ad beh·sur·yer...*

Dentist

I've broken a tooth/lost a filling.	**Jeg har brækket en tand/tabt en plombe.** *yie hah bray·gerdh ehn tan/tabt ehn ploam·ber*
I have a toothache.	**Jeg har tandpine.** *yie hah tan· pee·ner*
Can you fix this denture?	**Kan du reparere min protese?** *kan doo reh·pah·reh·ah meen proa·teh·ser*

Gynecologist

I have menstrual cramps/a vaginal infection.	**Jeg har menstruationssmerter/underlivsbetændelse.** *yie hah mehn·stroo·a shoans· smehr·dah/oa·nah·lee vs·beh·teh·nel·ser*
I missed my period.	**Jeg har ikke fået min menstruation.** *yie hah ig·ger fow·erdh meen mehn·stroo·a·shoan*
I'm on the Pill.	**Jeg tager p-piller.** *yie tah p eh·pil·lah*
I'm (...months) pregnant.	**Jeg er (...måneder) henne.** *yie ehr (...maw·nedh·ar) heh·ner*
I'm (not) pregnant.	**Jeg er (ikke) gravid.** *yie ehr (ig·ger) grah·veedh*
I haven't had my period for...months.	**Jeg har ikke haft menstruation i... måneder.** *yie hah ig·ger hahft mehn·stroo·a· shoan ee...mow·ner·dhah*

For Numbers, see page 159.

Optician

I've lost...	**Jeg har tabt....** *yie hah tahbt...*
a contact lens	**en af mine kontaktlinser** *ehn a <u>mee</u>·ner kohn·<u>tahkt</u>·lin·sah*
my glasses	**mine briller** *<u>mee</u>·ner bril·lah*
a lens	**en kontaktlinse** *ehn kohn·<u>tahkt</u>·lin·ser*

Payment & Insurance

How much?	**Hvor meget koster det?** *voar <u>mie</u>·erdh <u>kohs</u>·dah deh*
Can I pay by credit card?	**Kan jeg betale med kreditkort?** *kan yie beh·<u>ta</u>·ler mehdh kreh·<u>deet</u>·kawd*
I have insurance.	**Jeg er forsikret.** *yie ehr foh·<u>sik</u>·rerdh*
Can I have a receipt for my insurance?	**Må jeg få en kvittering til min sygeforsikring?** *mow yie fow ehn kvee·<u>teh</u>·ring til meen <u>sew</u>·er·foh·sik·ring*

Pharmacy

In Denmark, an **apotek** (pharmacy) fills medical prescriptions, while a **parfumeri** sells non-prescription items, such as toiletries and cosmetics. Regular hours are Monday to Thursday from 9:00 a.m. to 5:30 p.m. Pharmacies may close at 7:00 p.m. on Fridays and 1:00 p.m. on Saturdays. At other times, they work on a rotating schedule. Check the store window to find the closest pharmacy open.

What to Take

How much should I take?	**Hvor meget skal jeg tage?** *voar mie·erdh skal yie ta*
How often?	**Hvor ofte?** *voar ohf·der*
Is it suitable for children?	**Egner det sig til børn?** *ie·nah deh sie til burn*
I'm taking...	**Jeg tager...** *yie tah...*
Are there side effects?	**Er der nogen bivirkninger?** *ehr dehr noa·ern bee·veerk·ning·ah*
I'd like some medicine for...	**Jeg vil gerne have noget mod...** *yie vil gehr·ner ha n oa·erdh moadh...*
a cold	**forkølelse** *foh·kur·lerl·ser*
a cough	**hoste** *hoa·ster*
diarrhea	**diarré** *dee·a·reh*
a headache	**hovedpine** *hoh·ed·peeh·ner*
insect bites	**insektbid** *in·segt·beedh*
motion sickness	**køresyge** *kur·ah·sew·er*
a sore throat	**øm hals** *urm hals*
sunburn	**solforbrænding** *soal·foh·breh·ning*
a toothache	**tandpine** *tan·peeh·ner*
an upset stomach	**dårlig mave** *daw·lee ma·ver*

YOU MAY SEE...

EN GANG/TRE GANGE DAGLIGT	once/three times a day
PILLER	tablets
DRÅBER	drops
TESKEER	teaspoons
FØR/EFTER/I FORBINDELSE	before/after
MED ET MÅLTID	with meals
PÅ TOM MAVE	on an empty stomach
SLUG DEM HELE	swallow whole
KAN VIRKE DØSENDE	may cause drowsiness
KUN TIL UDVORTES BRUG	for external use only

Basic Supplies

I'd like...	**Jeg vil gerne have...** *yie vil <u>gehr</u>•ner ha...*
acetaminophen [paracetamol]	**en æske paracetamol** *ehn <u>ehs</u>•ker pah•rah•seh•ta•<u>moal</u>*
antiseptic cream	**en antiseptisk creme** *ehn <u>an</u>•tee•sehp•tisk krehm*
aspirin	**en æske hovedpinepiller** *ehn <u>ehs</u>•ger ho•wed•pee•ner•pil•lah*
bandages [plasters]	**noget plaster** *<u>noa</u>•erdh <u>plas</u>•dah*
a comb	**en kam** *ehn kahm*
condoms	**nogle kondomer** *<u>noa</u>•ler kohn•<u>doa</u>•mah*
contact lens solution	**noget kontaküinsevæske** *<u>noa</u>•erdh kohn•<u>tahkt</u>•lin•ser•vehs•ger*
deodorant	**deodorant** *deh•oa•doa•<u>rahnt</u>*
a hairbrush	**en hårbørste** *ehn haw•burr•sder*
hairspray	**noget hårlak** *<u>noa</u>•erdh <u>haw</u>•lahk*
ibuprofen	**en æske ibuprofen** *ehn <u>ehs</u>•ger ee•boo•proa•fehn*
insect repellent	**en insekt-spray** *ehn in•<u>sehkt</u>•spray*

a nail file	**en neglefil** *ehn <u>nie</u>·ler·f eel*	
a (disposable) razor	**en barberskraber** *ehn bah·<u>behr</u>·skrah·bah*	
razor blades	**nogle barberblade** <u>noa</u>·ler bah·<u>behr</u>·bla·dher	
sanitary napkins [towels]	**nogle hygiejnebind** <u>noa</u>·ler hew·gee·ie·ner·bin	
shampoo/ conditioner	**noget shampoo/hårbalsam** noa·erdh <u>shahm</u>·poa/<u>haw</u>·bal·sahm	
soap	**et stykke sæbe** *eht <u>stur</u>·ger <u>say</u>·ber*	
sunscreen	**noget solcreme** <u>noa</u>·erdh <u>soal</u>·krehm	
tampons	**nogle tamponer** <u>noa</u>·ler tahm·<u>pong</u>·ah	
tissues	**nogle papirlommetørklæder** <u>noa</u>·ler pah·<u>peer</u>·loh·mer·tu r·kl ay·dhah	
toilet paper	**noget toiletpapir** <u>noa</u>·erdh toa·ee·<u>leht</u>·pah·peer	
I'd like...	**Jeg vil gerne have...** *yie vil <u>gehr</u>·ner ha...*	
a toothbrush	**en tandbørste** *ehn <u>tahn</u>·bur·ster*	
toothpaste	**noget tandpasta** <u>noa</u>·erdh <u>tahn</u>·pas·ta	

For Baby Essentials, see page 140.

The Basics

Grammar

Regular Verbs

The present tense of regular verbs in Danish is formed by adding -r to the infinitive. The past tense is formed by adding -de to the infinitive or -te to the root. The future is formed by using the present tense of **ville** (will) + the verb in the infinitive. This applies to all persons (e.g., I, you, he, she, it, etc.). Following are the present, past and future forms of the verbs **at snakke** (to speak) and **at spise** (to eat). The different conjugation endings are in bold.

	present	past	future
at snakke (to speak)	snakk**er**	snakke**de**	vil snakke
at spise (to eat)	spis**er**	spis**te**	vil spise

Pronouns	
I	**jeg**
you (sing. inf./for.)	**du/De**
he	**han**
she	**hun**
it (common/neuter)	**den/det**
we	**vi**
you (pl.)	**I**
they	**de**

Irregular Verbs

There are a number of irregular verbs in Danish; these must be memorized. Like regular verbs, however, the irregular verb form remains the same, irrespective of person. Following are the present, past and future conjugations for a number of important, useful irregular verbs.

for. =formal   inf. = informal

sing. = singular   pl. = plural

	present	past	future
at være (to be)	er	var	vil være
at have (to have)	har	havde	vil have
at kunne (to be able)	kan	kunne	vil kunne
at gå (to walk)	går	gik	vil gå
at tage (to take)	tager	tog	vil tage

Word Order

Danish is similar to English in terms of word order for simple sentences: It follows the subject-verb-object pattern.

Example: **Vi efterlader vores bagage her.** We leave our luggage here.

When the sentence doesn't begin with a subject, the word order changes; the verb and the subject are inverted.

Questions are formed by reversing the order of the subject and verb:

Du ser bilen.	You see the car.
Ser du bilen?	Do you see the car?

Negation

A statement can be negated by inserting the word **ikke** after the verb:

Jeg taler dansk. I speak Danish.

Jeg taler ikke dansk. I do not speak Danish.

Imperatives

The imperative is exactly the same form as the stem of the verb:

Rejs!	Travel!	**Gå!**	Walk!
Tro!	Believe!	**Spis!**	Eat!

Nouns & Articles

The indefinite article (a, an) is expressed with **en** for common nouns and with **et** for neuter nouns. Generally, common nouns are those that can be both feminine and masculine (e.g. people, animals, etc.); neuter nouns have no gender (e.g. house, roof, etc.). However, note that there are several exceptions to this rule. Indefinite plurals are formed by adding **-e, -r** or **-er** to the singular.

	singular		plural	
common	**en pige**	a girl	**piger**	girls
neuter	**et hus**	a house	**huse**	houses

Some nouns remain unchanged in the plural, for example:

et rum	a room
rum	rooms

Definite articles: Where in English we say 'the car', the Danes say the equivalent of 'car-the', i.e. they tag the definite article onto the end of the noun. In the singular, common nouns take an **-en** ending, neuter nouns an **-et** ending. In the plural, both take an **-(e)ne** or **-(er)ne** ending.

	singular		plural	
common	**kanin**	the rabbit	**kaninerne**	the rabbits
neuter	**toget**	the train	**togene**	the trains

Adjectives

Adjectives usually precede nouns. In certain circumstances, the adjective takes an ending. In the singular indefinite form, adjectives remain unchanged but, in the plural indefinite form, with both common and neuter nouns, the adjective takes an **-e** ending.

singular		plural	
common	en stor bil	a big car	store bil**er**	big cars
neuter	et stort hus	a big house	store huse	big houses

In the definite form, an adjective takes an **-e** ending with both common and neuter nouns, in both the singular and plural. However, in this definite usage, **den** must be placed in front of the adjective in the case of common nouns in the singular, **det** in the case of singular neuter nouns and **de** with any plural.

	singular		plural	
common	**den** store bil	the big car	**de** stor **e** biler	the big cars
neuter	**det** store hus	the big house	**de** store huse	the big houses

Adverbs and Adverbial Expressions

Adverbs are generally formed by adding **-t** to the corresponding adjective.

Hun går hurtigt.	She walks quickly.
Hun går en hurtig tur.	She has a quick walk.

Numbers

ESSENTIAL

0	**nul**	*noal*
1	**en**	*ehn*
2	**to**	*toa*
3	**tre**	*treh*
4	**fire**	*fee·ah*
5	**fem**	*fehm*
6	**seks**	*sehks*
7	**syv**	*sew*
8	**otte**	*oa·der*
9	**ni**	*nee*
10	**ti**	*tee*
11	**elleve**	*ehl·ver*
12	**tolv**	*toal*
13	**tretten**	*treh·dern*
14	**fjorten**	*fyoar·dern*
15	**femten**	*fehm·dern*
16	**seksten**	*sie·stern*
17	**sytten**	*sur·dern*

18	**atten** _a_·dern
19	**nitten** _ni_·dern
20	**tyve** _tew_·ver
21	**enogtyve** _ehn_·oh·tew·ver
22	**tooggyve** _toa_·oh·tew·ver
30	**tredive** _trehdh_·ver
31	**enogtredive** _ehn_·oh·trehdh·ver
40	**fyrre** _fur_·er
50	**halvtreds** hal·_trehs_
60	**tres** trehs
70	**halvfjerds** hal·_fyehrs_
80	**firs** feers
90	**halvfems** hal·_fehms_
100	**hundrede** _hoon_·rah·dher
101	**hundrede og et** _hoon_·rah·dher ow eht
200	**to hundrede** toa _hoon_·rah·dher
500	**fem hundrede** fehm _hoon_·rah·dher
1000	**tusind** _too_·sin
10,000	**ti tusind** tee _too_·sin
1,000,000	**en million** ehn meel·_yoan_

Ordinal Numbers

first	**første** _furs_·der
second	**anden/andet** _an_·ern/_an_·erdh
third	**tredje** _trehdh_·yer
fourth	**fjerde** _fyay_·ah
fifth	**femte** _fehm_·der
once	**en gang** ehn gahng
twice	**to gange** toa _gahng_·er
three times	**tre gange** treh _gahng_·er

Time

ESSENTIAL

What time is it?	**Hvad er klokken?** *vadh ehr kloh·gern*
It's noon [midday].	**Klokken er tolv.** *kloh·gern ehr tohl*
At midnight.	**Ved midnat.** *vedh meedh·nat*
From nine o'clock to five o'clock.	**Fra klokken ni til sytten.** *frah kloh·gern nee til surd·den*
Twenty after [past] four.	**Tyve minutter over fire.** *tew·ver mee·noo·dah ow·ah fee·ah*
A quarter to nine.	**Kvart i ni.** *kvaht ee nee*
5:30 a.m./p.m.	**Halv seks om morgenen/aftenen.** *hal sehks ohm moh·nern/af·tern*

Days

ESSENTIAL

Monday	**mandag** *man·da*
Tuesday	**tirsdag** *teers·da*
Wednesday	**onsdag** *oans·da*
Thursday	**torsdag** *tohs·da*
Friday	**fredag** *freh·da*
Saturday	**lørdag** *lur·da*
Sunday	**søndag** *surn·da*

Dates

yesterday	**i går** *ee gaw*
today	**i dag** *ee da*
tomorrow	**i morgen** *ee mohn*
day	**dag** *da*
week	**uge** *oo•er*
month	**måned** *mow•nerdh*
year	**år** *aw*

Denmark follows a day-month-year format instead of the month-day-year format used in the U.S.
E.g.: July 25, 2008; 25/07/08 = 7/25/2008 in the U.S.

Months

January	**januar** *ya•noo•ah*
February	**februar** *feh•broo•ah*
March	**marts** *mahts*
April	**april** *a•preel*
May	**maj** *mie*
June	**juni** *yoo•nee*
July	**juli** *yoo•lee*
August	**august** *ow•goast*
September	**september** *sehp•tehm•bah*
October	**oktober** *ohk•toa•bah*
November	**november** *noa•vehm•bah*
December	**december** *deh•sehm•bah*

Seasons

spring	**forår** _foh_·aw
summer	**sommer** _sohm_·mah
fall [autumn]	**efterår** _ehf_·dah·aw
winter	**vinter** _vin_·dah

Holidays

January 1, New Year's Day	**Nytårsdag**
June 5, Constitution Day (afternoon only)	**Grundlovsdag**
December 24, Christmas Eve	**Juleaften**
December 25, Christmas Day	**Første juledag**
December 26, Boxing Day	**Anden juledag**
Maundy Thursday	**Skærtorsdag**
Good Friday	**Langfredag**
Easter Sunday	**Første påskedag**
Easter Monday	**Anden påskedag**
General Prayer Day	**Store Bededag**
Ascension Day	**Kristi himmelfart**

Conversion Tables

When you know	Multiply by	To find
ounces	28.3	grams
pounds	0.45	kilograms
inches	2.54	centimeters
feet	0.3	meters
miles	1.61	kilometers
square inches	6.45	sq. centimeters
square feet	0.09	sq. meters
square miles	2.59	sq. kilometers
pints (U.S./Brit)	0.47/0.56	liters
gallons (U.S./Brit)	3.8/4.5	liters
Fahrenheit	5/9, after 32	Centigrade
Centigrade	9/5, then +32	Fahrenheit

Kilometers to Miles Conversions

1 km	0.62 miles
5 km	3.1 miles
10 km	6.2 miles
50 km	31 miles
100 km	62 miles

Measurement

1 gram	**gram** _grahm_	= 0.035 oz.
1 kilogram (kg)	**kilo** _kee·loa_	= 2.2 lb
1 liter (l)	**liter** _lee·dah_	= 1.06 U.S./0.88 Brit. quarts
1 centimeter (cm)	**decimeter** _deh·see·meh·dah_	= 0.4 inch
1 meter (m)	**meter** _meh·dah_	= 3.28 feet
1 kilometer (km)	**kilometer** _kee·loa·meh·dah_	= 0.62 mile

Temperature

-40° C – -40° F	-1 ° C – 30° F	20° C – 68° F
-30° C – -22° F	0° C – 32° F	25° C – 77° F
-20° C – -4° F	5° C – 41 ° F	30° C – 86° F
-10° C – 14° F	10° C – 50° F	35° C – 95° F
-5° C – 23° F	15° C – 59° F	

Oven Temperature

100° C – 212° F	177° C – 350° F
121 ° C – 250° F	204° C – 400° F
149° C – 300° F	260° C – 500° F

Dictionary

moatdvilje (*moadh-vil-?er*) c
dislike; antipathy
mohair (moa-*hæer*) c mohair
mole (*moa-ler*) c jetty, pier
moment (moa-*mehnd*) *nt*
factor
momentan (moa-mehn-*tahn*)
adj momentary
monark (moa-*naag*) c
monarki (moa-*nah-ki*) *nt*
monarchy

A

a (with common nouns) en;
  (with neuter nouns) et
able kunne
about cirka
above ovenpå
accept *v* tage imod; **(approval)**
  godkende
access *n* adgang
accessory tilbehør
accident ulykke
account konto
ache smerte
acupuncture akupunktur
adapter adapter
address *n* adresse
admission adgang
admitted give adgang for
after efter
afternoon eftermiddag
aftershave lotion barbersprit
again igen
against mod
age alder
air conditioning klimaanlæg

air mattress luftmadras
airmail luftpost
airplane fly
airport lufthavn
aisle seat sæde ved midtergangen
alarm clock vækkeur
alcohol alkohol
alcoholic *adj* alkoholisk
allergic allergisk
allergic reaction allergisk reaktion
alphabet alfabet
also også
alter *v* ændre
altitude sickness bjergsyge
amazing forbløffende
amber rav
ambulance ambulance
American amerikaner
amethyst ametyst
amount *n* **(money)** beløb
amusement park forlystelsespark
analgesic smertestillende middel
and og
anesthetic narkose
animal dyr

| **adj** adjective | **BE** British English |
| **v** verb | **n** noun |

ankle ankel
answer svar
antibiotic antibiotikum
antidepressant antidepressivt
　middel
antique antikvitet
antiques store antikvitetshandler
antiseptic cream antiseptisk creme
any nogen
anyone nogen
anything noget
anywhere hvor som helst
apartment lejlighed
aperitif aperitif
appendix blindtarm
appliance udstyr
appointment aftale
arcade spillehal
architect arkitekt
arm arm
aromatherapy aromaterapi
around (approximately) omkring;
　(around the corner) rundt om
arrival ankomst
arrive ankomme
art kunst
art gallery kunstgalleri
aspirin hovedpinepille
assistance hjælp
assorted blandet
asthma astma

astringent sammentrækkende
　middel
at ved
ATM pengeautomat
attack *n* overfald
attend deltage
attractive køn
audio guide lydguide
Australia Australien
average gennemsnitlig
away væk
awful skrækkelig

B

baby baby
baby bottle sutteflaske
baby food babymad
baby wipes vådservietter
babysitter babysitter
back ryg
backache rygsmerter
backpack rygsæk
bad dårlig
bag (purse) taske; **(shopping)** pose
baggage [BE] bagage
baggage check bagageopbevaring
baggage claim bagagebånd
bakery bageri
balance (finance) saldo
balcony altan
ballet ballet

bandage *n* plaster
bank (finance) bank
bank note seddel
bar bar
barber herrefrisør
basket kurv
basketball game basketballkamp
bath bad
bathing suit badedragt
bathrobe badekåbe
bathroom badeværelse
battery batteri
battleground kampplads
be være
beach ball badebold
beard skæg
beautiful smuk
beauty salon skønhedssalon
bed seng
before (time) før
begin begynde
behind bagved
beige beige
bell (electric) ringeklokke
below nedenunder
belt bælte
berth køje
better bedre
between mellem
bicycle cykel
big stor

bike route cykelsti
bikini bikini
bill (restaurant) regning; **(bank note)** seddel
binoculars kikkert
bird fugl
birth fødsel
birthday fødselsdag
black sort
bladder blære
blade barberblad
blanket tæppe
bleach blegning
bleed bløde
blind (window) rullegardin
blister blist
blocked stoppet
blood blod
blood pressure blodtryk
blouse bluse
blow dry føntørre
blue blå
boat båd
boat trip bådtur
body krop
bone knogle
book bog
booklet (of tickets) rabatkort
bookstore boghandel
boot støvle
boring kedelig

born født
botanical garden botanisk have
botany botanik
bother genere
bottle flaske
bottle opener oplukker
bottom forneden
bowel tarm
bowl skål
box æske
boxing match boksekamp
boy dreng
boyfriend kæreste
bra bh
bracelet armbånd
brake *n* bremse
break (out of order) være i uorden
breakdown (car) få motorstop
breakfast morgenmad
breast bryst
breathe trække vejret
bridge bro
bring tage med
bring down få ned
British (person) brite; *adj* britisk
broken i stykker
brooch broche
broom kost
brown brun
bruise blåt mærke
brush *n* børste

bucket spand
bug insekt
build bygge
building bygning
burn brandsår
bus bus
bus station busstation
bus stop busholdeplads
business card visitkort
business center (at hotel)
   businesscenter
business class business class
business district forretningskvarter
business trip forretningsrejse
busy optaget
but men
butane gas flaskegas
butcher slagter
button knap
buy købe

C

cabin (ship) kahyt
cafe café
calculator regnemaskine
calendar kalender
call *n* **(phone)** opringning; *v* ringe;
   (summon) ringe efter
calm rolig
camera kamera
camera case fototaske

camera shop fotoforretning
camp bed campingseng
camp v campere
camping camping
camping equipment campingudstyr
campsite campingplads
can opener dåseåbner
can v (be able to) kan; n (container) dåse
Canada Canada
Canadian canadier
cancel annullere
candle stearinlys
candy store slikbutik
cap kasket
car bil
car hire [BE] biludlejning
car mechanic bilmekaniker
car park [BE] parkeringsplads
car rental biludlejning
car seat barnesæde
carafe karaffel
card kort
card game kortspil
cardigan cardigan
carry bære
cart indkøbsvogn
carton (of cigarettes) karton
case (camera) taske
cash v Indløse; n kontant

cashier kasse
casino kasino
castle slot; borg
caution forsigtig
cave hule
CD cd
cell phone mobiltelefon
cemetery kirkegård
center of town centrum
centimeter centimeter
ceramics keramik
certain vis
certificate attest
chair stol
change n (money) byttepenge; v (money) veksle; v (clothes, diaper) skifte
charcoal trækul
charge n gebyr; v koste
cheap billig
check (restaurant) n regning; (banking) check; v (someone, something) kontrollere; (luggage) tjekke ind
check-in desk (airport) check-in skranke
checking account checkkonto
check out v tjekke ud
check-up (medical) undersøgelse
cheers skål
chef køkkenchef

chemical toilet kemisk toilet
chemist [BE] apotek
cheque [BE] check
chess skak
chess set skakspil
chest brystkasse
chest pain smerter i brystet
child barn
child's seat barnesæde
children's clothing børnetøj
children's portion børneportion
choice valg
church kirke
cigar cigar
cigarette cigaret
cinema [BE] biograf
classical klassisk
clean adj ren; v gøre rent
cleansing cream rensecreme
clear v slette
cliff klippe
clip clips
clock ur
close v lukke
closed lukket
cloth stof
clothing tøj
clothing store tøjbutik
cloud sky
coat n (**clothing**) frakke
coin mønt

cold (illness) forkølelse; adj kold
collar flip
colleague kollega
color farve
comb kam
come komme
comedy lystspil
commission (fee) kommission
common (frequent) almindelig
compartment (train) kupé
compass kompas
complaint klage
computer computer; pc
concert koncert
concert hall koncertsal
condom kondom
conference room mødelokale
confirm bekræfte
confirmation bekræftelse
congratulations til lykke
connect v koble sig på
connection (transportation, internet) forbindelse
constipation forstoppelse
consulate konsulat
contact lens kontaktlinse
contagious smitsom
contain indeholde
contraceptive præventivmiddel
contract kontrakt
control kontrol

convention hall konferencesal
cooking facilities køkkenfaciliteter
copper kobber
corkscrew proptrækker
corner hjørne
cost n omkostning; v koste
cot klapseng
cotton bomuld
cough n hoste
counter disk
country land
countryside på landet
court house retsbygning
cover charge beregning per kuvert
cramps krampe
crayon farveblyant
cream (toiletry) creme
credit kredit
credit card kreditkort
crib barneseng
crockery [BE] spisestel
cross-country skiing langrend
crossing (maritime) overfart
crossroads vejkryds
crown (Danish currency) krone
crystal krystal
cufflink manchetknap
cuisine køkken
cup kop
currency valuta
currency exchange office
   vekselkontor
current (ocean) strøm
curtain gardin
customs told
customs declaration form
   toldangivelsesformular
cut n **(wound)** snitsår; v **(with
   scissors)** klippe
cut glass slebet glas
cycling race cykelløb

D

dairy mejeri
damaged beskadiget
dance club diskotek
dance n dans; v danse
danger fare
dangerous farlig
Danish (person) dansker; adj dansk
dark mørk
date (appointment) stævnemøde;
   (day) dato
day dag
decision beslutning
deck (ship) dæk
deck chair liggestol
declare (customs) fortolde
deep dyb
degree (temperature) grad
delay forsinkelse
delicatessen delikatesseforretning

delicious dejlig
deliver levere
delivery levering
denim denim
Denmark Danmark
dentist tandlæge
denture protese
deodorant deodorant
depart afgå
department (shop) afdeling
department store stormagasin
departure afgang
departure gate afgangsgate
deposit *n* **(bank)** indskud; **(down payment)** depositum
dessert dessert
detergent opvaskemiddel
detour (traffic) omkørsel
diabetic diabetiker
diamond diamant
diaper ble
diarrhea diarré
dictionary ordbog
diesel diesel
diet kost
difficult svær
digital digital
dining car spisevogn
dining room spisesalen
dinner middag

direct *adj* direkte; *v* **(someone)** vise vej til
direction vejangivelse
directory (phone) telefonbog
dirty beskidt
disabled handicappet
disc (parking) parkeringsskive
disconnect *v* **(computer)** koble sig fra
discount rabat
disease sygdom
dish (food item) ret
dishes (plates) spisetallerkner
dishwasher opvaskemaskine
dishwashing detergent opvaskemiddel
disinfectant desinficeringsmiddel
display case udstillingsmontre
district (of town) kvarter
disturb forstyrre
divorced skilt
dizzy svimmel
doctor læge
doctor's office lægekonsultation
dog hund
doll dukke
dollar (U.S.) dollar
domestic (airport terminal) indenrigs
domestic flight indenrigsfly
double bed dobbeltseng

double room dobbeltværelse

down ned

downtown area indre by

dozen dusin

dress n kjole

drink n drikkevare; **(cocktail)** drink; v drikke

drinking water drikkevand

drip dryppe

drive køre

driver's license kørekort

drop (liquid) dråbe

drugstore apotek

dry tør

dry cleaner renseri

dummy [BE] (baby's) sut

during i løbet af

duty (customs) told

duty-free goods toldfri varer

duty-free shop toldfri butik

dye farvning

E

each hver

ear øre

ear drops øredråber

earache ondt i ørerne

early tidligt

earring ørenring

east øst

easy nem

eat spise

economy class økonomiklasse

elastic elastik

electric elektrisk

electrical outlet stikkontakt

electricity elektricitet

electronic elektronisk

elevator elevator

e-mail e-mail

e-mail address e-mail-adresse

embassy ambassade

embroidery broderi

emerald smaragd

emergency nødstilfælde

emergency exit nødudgang

empty tom

enamel emalje

end slutning

engaged (phone) optaget

England England

English (language) engelsk; **(person)** englænder

enjoyable dejlig

enlarge forstørre

enough nok

enter v indtaste

entrance indgang

entrance fee entré

entry (access) adgang

envelope konvolut

equipment udstyr

eraser viskelæder
escalator rulletrappe
estimate *n* overslag; **(quotation)** tilbud
e-ticket e-billet
e-ticket check-in e-billet check-in
eurocheque eurocheck
Europe Europa
European Union Europæiske Fællesskab
evening aften
every hver
everything alt
exchange rate vekselkurs
exchange *v* **(money)** veksle
excursion udflugt
excuse *v* undskylde
exhibition udstilling
exit *n* udgang; *v* **(computer)** forlade
expect vente
expense udgift
expensive dyr
express ekspres
expression udtryk
extension (phone) lokal
extra ekstra
eye øje
eye drops øjendråber
eye shadow øjenskygge
eyesight syn

F

fabric (cloth) stof
face ansigt
facial ansigtsbehandling
factory fabrik
fair messe
fall *v* falde
family familie
fan ventilator
far langt
fare (ticket) billet
farm bondegård
far-sighted langsynet
fast *adj* hurtig
fast-food place burgerbar
faucet vandhane
fax fax
fax number faxnummer
fee (commission) kommission
feed *v* made
feel (physical state) føle
ferry færge
fever feber
few et par stykker
field mark
file (for nails) fil
fill in (form) udfylde
filling (tooth) plombe
film [BE] film
filter filter
find *v* finde

fine (OK) fint
fine arts kunst
finger finger
fire brand
fire door branddør
fire escape brandtrappe
fire exit nødudgang
first første
first-aid kit nødhjælpskasse
first class første klasse
first course forret
fishing fiskeri
fit v passe
fitting room prøverum
fix v reparere
flashlight lommelygte
flat [BE] (apartment) lejlighed
flatware bestik
flea market loppemarked
flight fly
floor etage
florist blomsterhandler
flower blomst
flu influenza
fluid væske
fog tåge
follow følge
food mad
food poisoning madforgiftning
foot fod
football [BE] fodbold

for for
forbidden forbudt
forecast vejrudsigt
foreign udenlandsk
forest skov
forget glemme
fork gaffel
form (document) formular
fountain springvand
frame (glasses) stel
free ledigt
freezer fryser
fresh frisk
friend ven
from fra
frost frostvejr
frying pan stegepande
full fuld
full-time fuldtids
furniture møbel

G

gallery galleri
game spil
garage garage
garbage skrald
garden have
gas benzin
gasoline benzin
gauze gaze
gem ædelsten

general almindelig
general delivery poste restante
general practitioner [BE]
  praktiserende læge
genuine ægte
get (find) komme til
get off stige af
get up stå op
gift gave
gift shop gavebutik
girl pige
girlfriend kæreste
give give
gland kirtel
glass (drinking) glas
glasses (optical) briller
glove handske
glue lim
go away gå væk
go back køre tilbage
go out gå ud
gold guld
golf club golfkølle
golf course golfbane
golf tournament golfturnering
good god
good afternoon goddag
good evening godaften
good morning godmorgen
good night godnat
goodbye farvel

gram gram
grandchild barnebarn
gray grå
great (excellent) storartet
Great Britain Storbritannien
green grøn
greengrocer's [BE] grønthandler
greeting hilsen
ground-floor room [BE] værelse i
  stueetagen
groundsheet teltunderlag
group gruppe
guesthouse pensionat
guide dog førerhund
guide n guide
guidebook rejsefører
gym motionscenter
gynecologist gynækolog

H

hair hår
hair dryer hårtørrer
hairbrush hårbørste
haircut klipning
hairdresser frisør
hairspray hårlak
hall (room) sal
hammer hammer
hammock hængekøje
hand hånd
hand cream håndcreme

hand washable vaske i hånden
handbag [BE] håndtaske
handicrafts kunsthåndværk
handkerchief lommetørklæde
handmade håndlavet
hanger bøjle
happy glad
harbor havn
hard hård
hardware store isenkræmmer
hare hare
hat hat
have (must) skulle; **(possess)** have
hay fever høfeber
head hoved
headache hovedpine
headlight billygte
headphones hovedtelefon
health food store helsekostforretning
health insurance sygeforsikring
hearing-impaired hørehæmmet
heart hjerte
heart attack hjerteanfald
heat v opvarme
heating varme
heavy tung
hello hej
helmet hjelm
help hjælp; **(oneself)** tage selv
here her

hi hej
high adj høj
high tide flod
highchair høj stol
highway motorvej
hill bakke
hire [BE] v leje
history historie
hole hul
holiday helligdag; **[BE]** ferie
home hjem
horseback riding ridning
hospital hospital
hot (temperature) varm
hotel hotel
hotel directory hotelfortegnelse
hotel reservation værelsesbestillig
hour (time) time
house hus
how hvordan
how far hvor langt
how long hvor længe
how many hvor mange
how much hvor meget
hug v kramme
hungry sulten
hunting jagt
hurry travlt
hurt gøre ondt
husband mand

I jeg
ice is
icy (weather) iskoldt
identification (card) id-kort
if hvis
ill [BE] syg
illness sygdom
important vigtig
imported importeret
impressive imponerende
in i
include iberegne
indoor indendørs
inexpensive billig
infected betændt
infection betændelse
inflammation betændelse
information information
information desk informationsluge
injection indsprøjtning
injure komme til skade
injury kvæstelse
inn kro
innocent uskyldig
inquiry forespørgsel
insect bite insektbid
insect repellent insekt-spray
insect spray insekt-spray
inside indenfor
instant messenger instant

messenger
insurance forsikring
insurance claim forsikringskrav
interest (finance) rente
interested interesseret
interesting interessant
international international; (airport
    terminal) udenrigs
international flight udenrigsfly
internet internet
internet cafe internetcafé
interpreter tolk
intersection vejkryds
introduce præsentere
introduction (social) præsentation
investment investering
invitation indbydelse
invite v indbyde
invoice faktura
iodine jod
Ireland Irland
Irish (person) irlænder, *adj* irsk
iron n (clothing) strygejern; v stryge
itemized bill udspecificeret regning

J

jacket jakke
jar (container) glas
jaw kæbe
jazz jazz
jeans cowboybukser

jet ski jetski
jeweler guldsmed
join *v* komme med
joint (anatomy) led
journey rejse
just (only) bare

K

keep beholde
kerosene petroleum
key nøgle
key card nøglekort
kiddie pool børnebassin
kidney nyre
kilogram kilogram
kilometer kilometer
kind *adj* rar; *n* slags
kiss *v* kysse
knee knæ
knife kniv
knitwear strikvarer
knock banke på
know vide

L

label etiket
lace blonde
lactose intolerant laktoseintolerant
lake sø
lamp lampe
landscape landskab

language sprog
lantern lygte
large stor
last sidst
late (time) sent; **(delay)** forsinket
laugh grine
launderette [BE] møntvaskeri
laundromat møntvaskeri
laundry vasketøj
laundry facilities vaskerum
laundry service vaskeri
lawyer advokat
laxative afføringsmiddel
leather læder
leave *v* afgå; **(behind)** efterlade
left til venstre
left-luggage office [BE]
  bagageopbevaring
leg ben
lens (camera) objektiv; **(glasses)**
  linse
less mindre
lesson undervisning
letter brev
library bibliotek
license (driving) kørekort
life boat redningsbåd
life guard (beach) livredder
life jacket redningsvest
life preserver redningsbælte
lift [BE] elevator

light (color) lys; **(weight)** let
light bulb pære
lighter lighter
lightning lyn
like vil gerne; **(please)** kan lide
linen lærred
lip læbe
lipstick læbestift
liquor store vinhandel
listen høre på
liter liter
little (amount) en smule
live v bo
loafers hyttesko
local lokal
log off logge af
log on logge på
login log ind
long lange
long-sighted [BE] langsynet
look v se
lose miste
loss tab
lost faret vild
lost and found hittegodskontor
lost property office [BE]
  hittegodskontor
lotion lotion
loud (voice) høj
love v elske
lovely dejlig

low lav
low tide ebbe
luck lykke
luggage bagage
luggage cart bagagevogn
luggage locker bagageboks
lunch frokost
lung lunge

M

magazine blad
magnificent storartet
maid stuepige
mail n post; v poste
mailbox postkasse
make-up n sminke
mall butikscenter
mallet kølle
man mand
manager direktør
manicure manicure
many mange
map kort
market n market
married gift
mass (religious service) messe
massage massage
match n **(sport)** kamp
material stof
matinée eftermiddagsforestilling
mattress madras

may *v* må
meadow eng
meal måltid
mean *v* betyde
measure tage mål af
measuring cup målekrus
measuring spoon måleske
mechanic mekaniker
medicine (drug) medicin
meet mødes
memorial mindesmærke
memory card hukommelseskort
mend reparere
menu menu; menukort
message besked
meter meter
middle midten
midnight midnat
mileage kilometerpenge
minute minut
mirror spejl
miscellaneous forskellig
Miss frøken
miss *v* **(lacking)** mangle
mistake fejltagelse
mobile phone [BE] mobiltelefon
moisturizing cream
  fugtighedscreme
moment øjeblik
money penge
money order postanvisning

month måned
monument monument
moon måne
mop *n* moppe
moped knallert
more mere
morning morgen
mosque moské
mosquito net myggenet
motel motel
motorboat motorbåd
motorcycle motorcykel
motorway [BE] motorvej
moustache overskæg
mouth mund
mouthwash mundvand
move *v* flytte
movie film
Mr. hr.
Mrs. fru
much meget
mug *n* krus
mugging overfald
muscle muskel
museum museum
music musik
musical musical
must (have to) måtte

N

nail (body) negl

nail clippers negleklipper
nail file neglefil
nail salon neglesalon
name navn
napkin serviet
nappy [BE] ble
narrow smal
nationality nationalitet
natural naturlig
nausea kvalme
near nær
nearby i nærheden
near-sighted nærsynet
neck hals
necklace halskæde
need *v* brug for
needle nål
nerve nerve
never aldrig
new ny
newspaper avis
newsstand aviskiosk
next næste
next to ved siden af
nice (beautiful) dejlig
night nat
no nej
noisy støjende
none ingen
non-smoking ikke-ryger
noon middag

normal normal
north nord
nose næse
not ikke
note (bank note) seddel
notebook notesbog
nothing ikke noget
notice (sign) skilt
notify underrette
novice begynderniveau
now nu
number nummer
nurse sygeplejerske

O

o'clock klokken
occupation stilling
occupied optaget
office kontor
off-licence [BE] vinhandel
oil spiseolie
old gammel
old town gamle bydel
on på
on time til tiden
once en gang
one-way ticket enkeltbillet
only kun
open *adj* åben; *v* åbne
opera opera
operation operation

operator telefonist
opposite overfor
optician optiker
or eller
orange (color) orange
orchestra orkester; **(seats)** parket
order n bestilling; v bestille
out of order virker ikke
out of stock udsolgt
outlet (electric) stikkontakt
outside udenfor
oval oval
overlook n udkigspost
oxygen treatment
  oxygenbehandling

P

pacifier (baby's) sut
packet pakke
pad (sanitary) hygiejnebind
pail spand
pain smerte
painkiller smertestillende middel
paint n maling; v male
painting maleri
pair par
pajamas pyjamas
palace slot
palpitations hjertebanken
pants bukser
panty hose strømpebukser

paper papir
paper towel papirhåndklæde
parcel [BE] pakke
parents forældre
park n park; v parkere
parking parkering
parking disc parkeringsskive
parking garage parkeringskælder
parking lot parkeringsplads
parking meter parkometer
part del
part-time deltid
party (social gathering) fest
passport pas
passport control paskontrol
passport photo pasfoto
paste (glue) klister
pastry shop konditori
patch lappe
path sti
patient patient
pattern mønster
pay betale
payment betaling
peak n **(mountain)** bjergtop
pearl perle
pedestrian fodgænger
pediatrician børnelæge
pedicure pedicure
peg (tent) pløk
pen pen; kuglepen

pencil blyant
pendant vedhæng
penicillin penicillin
per day per dag
per hour per time
per person per person
per week per uge
percentage procentsats
perfume parfume
perhaps måske
period (monthly) menstruation
permit n (fishing) fiskekort;
  (hunting) jagtkort
person person
personal personlig
petite petit
petrol [BE] benzin
pewter tinlegering
pharmacy apotek
phone card telefonkort
photo billede
photocopy n fotokopi
photograph n billede
photography fotografering
phrase vending
pick up v (go get) hente
picnic medbragt mad
picnic basket madkurv
piece stykke
pill pille
pillow pude

PIN pinkode
pin n (brooch) nål
pink lyserød
pipe pibe
place n sted
plane fly
planetarium planetarium
plaster [BE] (bandage) plaster
plastic plastic
plastic bag plasticpose
plastic wrap plastikfolie
plate tallerken
platform [BE] (station) perron
platinum platin
play n (theatre) stykke; v spille
playground legeplads
playpen kravlegård
please vær venlig
plug (electric) stik
plunger svuppert; vaskesuger
pneumonia lungebetændelse
pocket lomme
point of interest seværdighed
point v pege
poison gift
poisoning forgiftning
pole (ski) skistav; (tent) teltstang
police politi
police report politianmeldelse
police station politistation
pond dam

pool svømmebassin
porcelain porcelæn
port havn
portable transportabel
porter portier
portion portion
post [BE] n post; v poste
post office posthus
postage porto
postage stamp frimærke
postcard postkort
pot gryde
pottery pottemageri
pound (British currency, weight)
   pund
powder pudder
pregnant gravid
premium (gas) 98 oktan
prescribe skrive recept på
prescription recept
present n gave
press (iron) presse
pressure tryk
pretty køn
price pris
price-fixed menu dagens menu
print n (photo) aftryk; v
   (document) udskrive
private privat
profit n overskud
program (of events) program

pronounce v udtale
pronunciation n udtale
provide skaffe
pull v trække
pump pumpe
puncture punktering
purchase n køb; v købe
pure ren
purple violet
purse (handbag) håndtaske
push v skubbe
pushchair [BE] klapvogn
put sætte

Q

quality kvalitet
quantity mængde
question n spørgsmål
quick hurtig
quiet stille

R

race væddeløb
race track væddeløbsbane
racket (sport) ketsjer
radio radio
railway station [BE]
   jernbanestation
rain regnvejr
raincoat regnfrakke
rape n voldtægt

rash udslet
rate n (**exchange**) vekselkurs; (**price**) takst
razor barbermaskine
razor blade barberblad
ready færdig
real (genuine) ægte
rear bagerst
receipt kvittering
reception reception
receptionist receptionist
recommend anbefale
rectangular rektangulær
red rød
reduction rabat
refrigerator køleskab
refund v få pengene tilbage
regards hilsner
region område
registered mail anbefalet
registration indskrivning
regular (gas) 95 oktan
relationship forhold
reliable pålidelig
religion religion
rent v leje
rental udlejning
rental car udlejningsbil
repair n reparation; v reparere
repeat v gentage
report (theft) anmelde

request n anmodning; v anmode
required nødvendig
requirement forespørgsel
reservation reservation
reservations office pladsreserveringen
reserve bestille
reserved reserveret
rest n rest
restaurant restaurant
restroom toilet
retired pensioneret
return (come back) komme tilbage; (**give back**) returnere
return ticket [BE] returbillet
rib ribben
ribbon bånd
right (correct) rigtigt; (**direction**) til højre
ring (jewelry) ring; (**bell**) ringe på
river flod
road vej
road assistance hjælp på vejen
road map vejkort
road sign vejskilt
robbery tyveri
romantic romantisk
room (hotel) værelse; (**space**) plads
room number værelsesnummer
room service roomservice; service på værelset

room temperature rumtemperatur
rope reb
round rund
round (golf) runde
round-trip ticket returbillet
route rute
rowboat robåd
rubber (material) gummi
rubbish [BE] skrald
ruby rubin

S

safe n **(vault)** boks; **(not in danger)** sikker
safety pin sikkerhedsnål
sailboat sejlbåd
sale n salg; **(bargains)** udsalg
same samme
sand sand
sandal sandal
sanitary napkin hygiejnebind
sapphire safir
satin satin
saucepan kasserolle
saucer underkop
sauna sauna
save v gemme
savings account opsparingskonto
scarf tørklæde
scenery landskab
scenic route køn rute

school skole
scissors saks
scooter scooter
Scotland Skotland
screwdriver skruetrækker
sculpture skulptur
sea hav
season sæson
seat plads
seat belt sele
second sekund
second class anden klasse
second-hand shop marskandiser; genbrugsbutik
section afdeling
see se
sell sælge
send sende
senior citizen pensionist
sentence sætning
separated (relationship) separeret
serious alvorlig
serve (meal) servere
service (restaurant) betjening
set menu fast menu
sew sy
shampoo shampoo
shape form
sharp (pain) skarp
shave n barbering
shaving brush barberbørste

shaving cream barbercreme
shelf hylde
ship *n* skib; *v* forsende
shirt skjorte
shoe sko
shoe store skoforretning
shop *n* butik
shopping indkøb
shopping area indkøbscenter
shopping centre [BE] butikscenter
shopping mall butikscenter
short kort
shorts shorts
short-sighted [BE] kortsynet
shoulder skulder
shovel *n* skovl
show *n* show; *v* vise
shower (stall) bruser
shrine helgengrav
shut lukket
shutter (window) skodde
side side
sightseeing sightseeing
sightseeing tour rundtur
sign underskrive
sign (notice) skilt;
   v underskrive
signature underskrift
silk silke
silver sølv
silverware sølvtøj

since siden
sing synge
single *n* **(ticket)** enkeltbillet;
   (unmarried) ugift
single room enkeltværelse
size størrelse; **(clothes)** mål; **(shoes)**
   nummer
skate *v* skøjte
skating rink skøjtebane
skin hud
skirt nederdel
sky himmel
sleep *v* sove
sleeping bag sovepose
sleeping car sovevogn
sleeping pill sovepille
sleeve ærme
slice *n* skive
slide (photo) dias
slipper hjemmesko
slow langsom
small lille
smoke ryge
smoker ryger
snack mellemmåltid
snack bar snackbar
sneaker gummisko
snorkeling equipment
   snorkeludstyr
snow sne
soap sæbe

soccer fodbold
soccer match fodboldkamp
sock sok
socket (electric) stikkontakt
soft blød
sold out udsolgt
someone nogen
something noget
song sang
soon snart
sore (painful) øm
sore throat ondt i halsen
sorry beklager
sort (kind) slags
south syd
souvenir souvenir
souvenir shop souvenirbutik
spa spa
spatula spatel
speak v tale
special særlig
specialist specialist
speciality specialitet
spell v stave
spend bruge
spine rygrad
sponge svamp
spoon ske
sport sport
sporting goods store
  sportsforretning

sprained forstuvet
square (shape) firkantet
stadium stadium
staff personale
stain plet
stainless steel rustfrit stål
stairs trappe
stamp n (**postage**) frimærke; v
  (**ticket**) stemple
staple hæfteklamme
star stjerne
start begynde
starter [BE] (meal) forret
station (train) jernbanestation;
  (**subway**) S-togsstation
stationery store papirhandel
stay (trip) ophold; v (**remain**) blive;
  v (**reside**) bo
steal stjæle
sterling silver sterlingsølv
sting n stik; v stikke
stockings strømpe
stomach mave
stomachache mavepine
stop (bus) busholdeplads; v stop
store (shop) forretning
store directory butiksoversigt
stove ovn
straight ahead ligeud
strange underlig
street gade

street map gadekort
string snor
stroller klapvogn
strong stærk
student studerende
study v studere
stunning fantastisk flot
sturdy solid
subway metro
subway map togkort
suit (man's) habit; **(woman's)** dragt
suitcase kuffert
sun sol
sunburn solforbrænding
sunglasses solbriller
sunstroke solstik
sun-tan lotion solcreme
super (gas) 98 oktan
supermarket supermarked
supplement n tillæg
suppository stikpille
surgery [BE] lægekonsultation
surname efternavn
swallow sluge
sweater sweater
sweatshirt sweatshirt
sweet sød
swell hæve
swelling hævelse
swim v svømme
swimming svømning

swimming pool svømmebasin
swimming trunks badebukser
swollen hævet
symbol symbol
synagogue synagoge
synthetic syntetisk
system system

T

table bord
tablet (medical) pille
tailor skrædder
take tage
take away v [BE] tage med
taken (occupied) taget
tampon tampon
tap (water) vandhane
tax skat
taxi taxa
taxi rank [BE] taxaholdeplads
taxi stand taxaholdeplads
team hold
tear v rive i stykker
teaspoon teske
telephone booth telefonboks
telephone directory telefonbog
telephone n telefon; v ringe
telephone number telefonnummer
tell sige
temperature temperatur
temple tempel

temporary midlertidig
tennis court tennisbane
tennis match tenniskamp
tennis racket tennisketsjer
tent telt
tent peg teltpløk
tent pole teltstang
terminal terminal
terrace terrasse
terrible frygtelig
terrifying skrækindjagende
thank takke
thank you tak
theater teater
theft tyveri
then så
there der
thermometer termometer
thief tyv
thigh lår
thin tynd
think (believe) tro
thirsty tørstig
thread tråd
throat hals
through gennem
thumb tommelfinger
thunder torden
thunderstorm tordenvejr
ticket billet
ticket office billetluge

tide ebbe
tie slips
tie clip slipseklemme
time *n* tid; **(recurrent occasion)**
    gang
timetable [BE] køreplan
tin [BE] (container) dåse
tin opener [BE] dåseåbner
tire dæk
tired træt
tissue papirslommetørklæde
to til
tobacco tobak
tobacconist tobakshandler
today i dag
toe tå
toilet [BE] toilet
toilet paper toiletpapir
toiletry toiletartikel
tomb gravsted
tomorrow i morgen
tongue tunge
tonight i aften
too (also) også
too much for meget
tool værktøj
tooth tand
toothache tandpine
toothbrush tandbørste
toothpaste tandpasta
torn (clothes) gået i stykker

touch v røre

tour tur

tourist office turistkontor

tow truck kranbil

towards mod

towel håndklæde

tower tårn

town by

town hall rådhus

toy legetøj

toy store legetøjsforretning

track (train) spor

traffic light trafiklys

trail gangsti

trailer campingvogn

train tog

tram sporvogn

tranquillizer beroligende middel

transfer (money) overførsel

translate oversætte

travel rejse

travel agency rejsebureau

travel guide rejsefører

travel sickness køresyge

traveler's check rejsecheck

treatment behandling

tree træ

trim studsning

trip rejse

trolley bagagevogn

trousers [BE] bukser

T-shirt T-shirt

tube tube

turn (change direction) drej til

turtleneck højhalset

TV fjernsyn

tweezers pincet

U

ugly grim

umbrella paraply; (beach) parasol

unconscious bevidstløs

under under

underground station [BE] metrostation

underpants underbukser

undershirt undertrøje

understand forstå

undress tage tøjet af

United States USA

university universitet

unleaded (fuel) blyfri

until indtil

up op

upstairs ovenpå

urgent haster

use brug

usually normalt

V

vacancy ledigt værelse

vacant ledig

vacation ferie
vaccinate vaccinere
vacuum cleaner støvsuger
valley dal
value værdi
value-added tax [BE] moms
vegetarian vegetar
vein vene
very meget
veterinarian dyrlæge
video camera videokamera
view (panorama) udsigt
village landsby
visit *n* besøg; *v* besøge
visiting hours besøgstid
visually impaired synshæmmet
V-neck V-hals
volleyball game volleyballkamp
voltage spænding
vomit *v* kaste op

W

wait *v* vente
waiter tjener
waiting room venteværelse
waitress kvindelig tjener
wake vække
wake-up call morgenvækning
Wales Wales
walk *n* gåtur
wall mur

wallet tegnebog
want vil have
warm (temperature) varm; *v*
   (reheat) opvarme
wash vaske
washing machine vaskemaskine
watch *n* ur
water vand
waterfall vandfald
waterproof vandtæt
water-ski vandski
wave *n* bølge
way vej
weather vejr
weather forecast vejrudsigt
week uge
weekend weekend
well godt
west vest
what hvad
wheel hjul
wheelchair kørestol
when hvornår
where hvor
which hvilken
white hvid
who hvem
whole hele
why hvorfor
wide brede
widow (female) enke; **(male)**

enkemand
wife kone
wind vind
window vindue; **(shop)** butiksvindue
window seat vinduessæde
windsurfer windsurfer
wine list vinliste
wireless trådløs
wish *v* ønske
with med
withdraw (banking) få udbetalt
without uden
woman kvinde
wonderful vidunderlig
wood skov
wool uld
word ord
work *v* virke
worse værre
wound sår
write skrive
wrong forkert

X

X-ray røntgenfotografere

Y

year år
yellow gul
yes ja
yesterday i går
yet endnu
young ung
youth hostel vandrehjem

Z

zipper lynlås
zoo zoologisk have

A

adapter adapter
adgang *n* access; admission; entry
adresse *n* address
advokat lawyer
afdeling *n* department (shop); section; entry
afføringsmiddel laxative
afgang departure
afgangsgate departure gate
afgå depart; leave
aftale appointment
aften evening
aftryk *n* print (photo)
akupunktur acupuncture
alder age
aldrig never
alfabet alphabet
alkohol alcohol
allergisk allergic
allergisk reaktion allergic reaction
almindelig common (frequent); general
alt everything
altan balcony
alvorlig serious
ambassade embassy
ambulance ambulance
amerikaner American

ametyst amethyst
anbefale recommend
anbefalet registered mail
anden klasse second class
ankel ankle
ankomme arrive
ankomst arrival
anmelde report (theft)
anmodning *n* request
annullere cancel
ansigt face
ansigtsbehandling facial
antibiotikum antibiotic
antidepressivt middel antidepressant
antikvitet antique
antikvitetshandler antiques store
antiseptisk creme antiseptic cream
apotek pharmacy [chemist BE]
arkitekt architect
arm arm
armbånd bracelet
aromaterapi aromatherapy
astma asthma
attest certificate
Australien Australia
automatgear automatic (car)
avis newspaper
aviskiosk newsstand

B

baby baby
babymad baby food
babysitter babysitter
bad bath
badebukser swimming trunks
badedragt bathing suit
badekåbe bathrobe
badeværelse bathroom
bagage luggage [baggage BE]
bagageboks luggage locker
bagagebånd baggage claim
bagageopbevaring baggage check
bagagevogn luggage cart [trolley BE]
bageri bakery
bagerst rear
bagved behind
bakke hill
ballet ballet
bane train
bank bank (finance)
banke på knock
bar bar
barberblad razor blade
barberbørste shaving brush
barbercreme shaving cream
barbering n shave
barbermaskine razor
barbersprit aftershave lotion
bare just (only)
barn child

barnebarn grandchild
barneseng crib
barnesæde car seat; child's seat
basketballkamp basketball game
batteri battery
bedre better
begynde begin; start
behandling treatment
beholde keep
beige beige
beklager sorry
bekræfte confirm
bekræftelse confirmation
beløb n amount (money)
ben leg
benzin gas [petrol BE]
beregning per kuvert cover charge
beroligende middel tranquillizer
beskadiget damaged
besked message
beskidt dirty
beslutning decision
bestik flatware
bestille v reserve; order
bestilling n order
besøg n visit
besøgstid visiting hours
betale pay
betaling payment
betjening service (restaurant)
betyde v mean

betændelse infection; inflammation
betændt infected
bevidstløs unconscious
bh bra
bibliotek library
bikini bikini
bil car
billede photo
billet ticket
billetluge ticket office
billig cheap
bilmekaniker car mechanic
biludlejning car rental [hire BE]
biograf movie theater [cinema BE]
bjergtop n peak (mountain)
blad magazine
blandet assorted
ble diaper [nappy BE]
blegning bleach
blindtarm appendix
blist blister
blod blood
blodtryk blood pressure
blomst flower
blomsterhandler florist
blonde lace
bluse blouse
blyant pencil
blyfri unleaded (fuel)
blød soft
bløde bleed

blå blue
blåt mærke bruise
bo v live
bog book
boghandel bookstore
boksekamp boxing match
bomuld cotton
bondegård farm
bord table
borg castle
botanisk have botanical garden
brand fire
branddør fire door
brandsår burn
brandtrappe fire escape
brede wide
bremse n brake
brev letter
briller glasses (optical)
brite British
bro bridge
broche brooch
broderi embroidery
brug use
brug for v need
bruge spend
brun brown
bruser n shower (stall)
bryst breast
brystkasse chest
bukser pants [trousers BE]

burgerbar fast-food place
bus bus
busholdeplads bus stop
business class business class
businesscenter business center (at hotel)
busstation bus station
butik *n* shop
butikscenter shopping mall [centre BE]
butiksoversigt store directory
by town
bygge build
bygning building
byttepenge *n* change (money)
bælte belt
bære carry
bøjle hanger
bølge *n* wave
børnebassin kiddie [paddling BE] pool
børnelæge pediatrician
børnemenu children's menu
børneportion children's portion
børnetøj children's clothing
børste *n* brush
båd boat
bådtur boat trip
bånd ribbon

C

café cafe
campere *v* camp
camping camping
campingplads campsite
campingseng camp bed
campingvogn trailer
Canada Canada
canadier Canadian
cardigan cardigan
cd CD
centimeter centimeter
centrum downtown area [centre BE]
check check [cheque BE] (banking)
check-in skranke check-in desk (airport)
checkkonto checking account
chokoladeforretning candy store
cigar cigar
cigaret cigarette
cirka about
clips clip
cowboybukser jeans
creme cream (toiletry)
cykel bicycle
cykelløb cycling race
cykelsti bike route

D

dag day
dagens menu price-fixed menu

dal valley
dam pond
dame lady
Danmark Denmark
dans *n* dance
dansk Danish (language, nationality)
dansker Danish (person)
dejlig delicious
del part
delikatesseforretning delicatessen
deltage attend
deltid part-time
denim denim
deodorant deodorant
der there
desinficeringsmiddel disinfectant
dessert dessert
diabetiker diabetic
diamant diamond
diarré diarrhea
dias slide (photo)
diesel diesel
direkte direct
direktør manager
disk counter
diskotek dance club
dobbeltseng double bed
dobbeltværelse double room
dollar dollar (U.S.)
drej til turn (change direction)
dreng boy

drikkevare *n* drink
dryppe drip
dråbe drop (liquid)
dukke doll
dusin dozen
dyb deep
dyr *adj* expensive; *n* animal
dyrlæge veterinarian
dæk deck (ship)
dårlig bad
dåse can [tin BE]
dåseåbner can [tin BE] opener

E

e-billet e-ticket
e-billet check-in e-ticket check-in
efter after
efterlade *v* leave (behind)
eftermiddag afternoon
eftermiddagsforestilling matinée
efternavn surname
ekspres express
ekstra extra
elastik *n* elastic
elektricitet electricity
elektrisk electric
elektronisk electronic
elevator elevator [lift BE]
eller or
elske *v* love
e-mail e-mail

e-mail-adresse e-mail address
emalje enamel
en a (with common nouns)
en gang once
en masse lot (a lot)
en smule little (amount)
endnu yet
eng meadow
engelsk English (language)
England England
englænder English (person)
enke widow (male)
enkemand widow (female)
enkeltbillet one-way [single BE] ticket
enkeltværelse single room
entré entrance fee
et a (with neuter nouns)
et par stykker few
etage floor
etiket label
eurocheck eurocheque
Europa Europe
Europæiske Fællesskab European Union

F

fabrik factory
faktura invoice
familie family
fantastisk flot stunning

fare danger
faret vild lost
farlig dangerous
farve color
farveblyant crayon
farvel goodbye
farvning dye
fast menu set menu
fax fax
faxnummer fax number
feber fever
fejltagelse mistake
ferie vacation
fest party (social gathering)
fil file (for nails)
film movie [film BE]
filter filter
finde find
finger finger
firkantet square (shape)
fiskekort *n* permit (fishing)
fiskeri fishing
fjernsyn TV
flaske bottle
flaskegas butane gas
flip collar
flod river; high tide
flonel flannel
fly airplane; flight
flytte *v* move
fod foot

fodbold soccer [football BE]
fodboldkamp soccer [football BE] match
fodgænger pedestrian
for for
for meget too much
for varm overheated (engine)
forbindelse connection (transportation, internet)
forbløffende amazing
forbudt forbidden
forældre parents
færdig ready
færge ferry
fødsel birth
fødselsdag birthday
født born
føle feel (physical state)
følge follow
føntørre blow-dry
før before (time)
førerhund guide dog
få motorstop breakdown (car)
få ned bring down
få pengene tilbage *v* refund
få udbetalt withdraw (banking)

G

gade street
gadekort street map
gaffel fork

galleri gallery
gamle bydel old town
gammel old
gang *n* time (recurrent occasion)
gangsti trail
garage garage
gardin curtain
gave gift; present
gavebutik gift shop
gaze gauze
gebyr *n* charge
gemme *v* save
genbrugsbutik second-hand shop
genere bother
gennem through
gennemsnitlig average
gentage *v* repeat
gift *adj* married; *n* poison
give give
give adgang for admitted
glad happy
glas glass; jar (container)
glemme forget
god good
godaften good evening
goddag good afternoon
godmorgen good morning
godnat good night
godt fine (OK); well
golfbane golf course
golfkølle golf club

golfturnering golf tournament
grad degree (temperature)
gram gram
grammatik grammar
gravid pregnant
gravsted tomb
grim ugly
grine laugh
gruppe group
gryde pot
grøn green
grønthandler produce store
  [greengrocer's BE]
grå gray
guide *n* guide
gul yellow
guld gold
guldsmed jeweler
gummi rubber (material)
gummisko sneaker
gynækolog gynecologist
gøre ondt hurt
gøre rent *v* clean
gå ud go out
gå væk go away
gåtur *n* walk

H

hals neck; throat
halskæde necklace
hammer hammer

handicappet disabled
handske glove
hare hare
haste urgent
hat hat
hav sea
have garden
havn harbor; port
hej hello; hi
hele whole
helgengrav shrine
helligdag holiday (public)
helsekostforretning health food
  store
hente *v* pick up (go get)
her here
herrefrisør barber
hilsen greeting
hilsner regards
himmel sky
historie history
hittegodskontor lost and found
  [lost property office BE]
hjelm helmet
hjem home
hjemmesko slipper
hjerte heart
hjerteanfald heart attack
hjertebanken palpitations
hjul wheel
hjælp assistance; help

hjælp på vejen roadside assistance
hjørne corner
hold team
hospital hospital
hoste *n* cough
hotel hotel
hotelfortegnelse hotel directory
hoved head
hovedpine headache
hovedpinepille aspirin
hovedtelefon headphones
hr. Mr.
hud skin
hukommelseskort memory card
hul hole
hule cave
hund dog
hurtig *adj* fast; quick
hus house
husholdningsartikel household item
hvad what
hvem who
hver each; every
hvid white
hvilken which
hvis if
hvor where
hvor langt how far
hvor længe how long
hvor mange how many

hvor meget how much
hvor som helst anywhere
hvordan how
hvorfor why
hvornår when
hygiejnebind sanitary napkin [pad BE]
hylde shelf
hyttesko loafers
hæfteklamme staple
hængekøje hammock
hæve swell
hævelse swelling
hævet swollen
høfeber hay fever
høj high; loud (volume)
høj stol highchair
højhalset turtleneck
høre på listen
hørehæmmet hearing impaired
hånd hand
håndcreme hand cream
håndklæde towel
håndlavet handmade
håndtaske purse [handbag BE]
hår hair
hårbørste hairbrush
hård hard
hårlak hairspray
hårtørrer hair dryer

I

i aften tonight
i dag today
i går yesterday
i løbet af during
i morgen tomorrow
i nærheden nearby
i stykker broken
iberegne include
id-kort identification (card)
igen again
ikke not
ikke noget nothing
ikke-ryger non-smoking
imponerende impressive
importeret imported
indbyde v invite
indbydelse invitation
indeholde contain
indendørs indoor
indenfor inside
indenrigs domestic (airport terminal)
indenrigsfly domestic flight
indgang entrance
indkøb shopping
indkøbscenter shopping area
indkøbsvogn cart
indløse v cash
indre by downtown area
indskrivning registration

indskud n deposit (bank)
indsprøjtning injection
indtaste v enter
indtil until
influenza flu
information information
informationsluge information desk
ingen none
insekt bug
insektbid insect bite
insekt-spray insect repellent
instant messenger instant messenger
interessant interesting
interesseret interested
international international (airport terminal)
internet internet
internetcafé internet cafe
investering investment
Irland Ireland
irlænder Irish
isenkræmmer hardware store
iskoldt icy (weather)

J

ja yes
jagt hunting
jakke jacket
jazz jazz
jeg I

jernbanestation train [railway BE] station

jetski jet ski

jod iodine

K

kahyt cabin (ship)

kalender calendar

kam comb

kamera camera

kamp *n* match (sport)

kampplads battleground

kan *v* can (be able to)

kapel chapel

karaffel carafe

karton carton (of cigarettes)

kasino casino

kasket cap

kasse cash desk; cashier

kasserolle saucepan

kedelig boring

kemisk toilet chemical toilet

keramik ceramics

ketsjer racket (sport)

kikkert binoculars

kilde *n* spring (water)

kilogram kilogram

kilometer kilometer

kilometerpenge mileage

kirke church

kirkegård cemetery

kirtel gland

kjole *n* dress

klage complaint

klapseng cot

klapvogn stroller [pushchair BE]

klassisk classical

klimaanlæg air conditioning

klipning haircut

klister paste (glue)

klokken o'clock

knallert moped

knap button

kniv knife

knogle bone

knæ knee

kobber copper

koble sig fra *v* disconnect (computer)

koble sig på *v* connect (computer)

kollega colleague

komme come

komme med join

komme til get (find)

komme til skade injure

komme tilbage return (give back)

kommission commission (fee)

kompas compass

koncert concert

koncertsal concert hall

konditori pastry shop

kondom condom

kone wife
konferencesal convention hall
konsulat consulate
kontaktlinse contact lens
konto account
kontor office
kontrakt contract
kontrol control
konvolut envelope
kop cup
kort card; map; *adj* short
kortspil card game
kortsynet near-sighted [short-sighted BE]
kost diet
kost broom
kramme *v* hug
krampe cramps
kranbil tow truck
kravlegård playpen
kredit credit
kreditkort credit card
kro inn
krone crown (Danish currency)
krop body
krus *n* mug (cup)
krystal crystal
kuffert suitcase
kuglepen pen
kun only
kunne able

kunst art
kunstgalleri art gallery
kunsthåndværk handicrafts
kupé compartment (train)
kurv basket
kvalitet quality
kvalme nausea
kvarter district (of town)
kvinde woman
kvindelig tjener waitress
kvittering receipt
kvæstelse injury
kysse *v* kiss
kæbe jaw
kæreste boyfriend; girlfriend
køb *n* purchase
købe buy
køje berth
køkken cuisine
køkkenchef chef
køkkenfaciliteter cooking facilities
køleskab refrigerator
kølle mallet
køn attractive; pretty
køn rute scenic route
køre drive
køre tilbage go back
kørekort driver's license
køreplan schedule [timetable BE]
kørestol wheelchair
køresyge travel sickness

L

laktoseintolerant lactose intolerant
lampe lamp
land country
landsby village
landskab landscape; scenery
lange long
langrend cross-country skiing
langsom slow
langsynet far-sighted
 [long-sighted BE]
langt far
lappe patch
lav low
led *n* joint (anatomy)
ledig vacant
ledigt free
ledigt værelse vacancy
legeplads playground
legetøj toy
legetøjsforretning toy store
leje *v* rent [hire BE]
lejlighed apartment [flat BE]
let light (weight)
levere deliver
levering delivery
ligeud straight ahead
liggestol deck chair
lighter lighter
lille small
lim glue

liter liter
livredder life guard (beach)
log ind login
logge af log off
logge på log on
lokal extension (phone); local
lomme pocket
lommelygte flashlight
lommetørklæde handkerchief
loppemarked flea market
lotion lotion
lufthavn airport
luftmadras air mattress
luftpost airmail
lukke *v* close
lunge lung
lungebetændelse pneumonia
lydguide audio guide
lygte lantern
lykke luck
lyn lightning
lynlås zipper
lys light (color)
lyserød pink
lystspil comedy
læbe lip
læbestift lipstick
læder leather
læge doctor
lægekonsultation doctor's office
 [surgery BE]

lærred linen
lår thigh

M

mad food
made v feed
madforgiftning food poisoning
madkurv picnic basket
madras mattress
maleri painting
maling n paint
manchetknap cufflink
mand husband; man
mange many
mangle v miss (lacking)
manicure manicure
mark field
marked market
marskandiser second-hand shop
massage massage
mave stomach
mavepine stomachache
med with
medbragt mad picnic
medicin medicine (drug)
meget much; very
mejeri dairy
mekaniker mechanic
mellem between
mellemmåltid snack
men but

menstruation period (menstrual)
menu menu
mere more
messe fair (event); mass (religious service)
meter meter
metro subway [underground BE]
metrostation subway [underground BE] station
middag dinner; noon
midlertidig temporary
midnat midnight
midten middle
mindesmærke memorial
mindre less
mindst at least
minut minute
miste lose
mobiltelefon cell [mobile BE] phone
mod against; toward
modtageren betaler call collect [reverse the charges BE]
moms sales tax [value-added tax BE]
monument monument
moppe n mop
morgen morning
morgenmad breakfast
morgenvækning wake-up call
moské mosque
motel motel
motionscenter gym

motorbåd motorboat
motorcykel motorcycle
motorvej highway [motorway BE]
mund mouth
mundvand mouthwash
mur wall
museum museum
musical musical
musik music
muskel muscle
myggenet mosquito net
mængde quantity
møbel furniture
mødelokale conference room
mødes meet
mønster pattern
mønt coin
møntvaskeri laundromat
   [launderette BE]
mørk dark
må may (can)
målekrus measuring cup
måleske measuring spoon
måltid meal
måne moon
måned month
måske perhaps
måtte must (have to)

N
narkose anesthetic

nat night
nationalitet nationality
naturlig natural
navn name
ned down
nedenunder below
nederdel skirt
negl nail (body)
neglefil nail file
negleklipper nail clippers
neglesalon nail salon
nej no
nem easy
nerve nerve
nogen any; anyone; someone; some
noget anything; some; something
nogle some
nok enough
nord north
normal adj normal
normalt adv usually
notesbog notebook
nu now
nummer number
ny new
nyre kidney
nær near
næse nose
næste next
nødhjælpskasse first-aid kit
nødstilfælde emergency

nødudgang emergency exit
nødvendig required
nøgle key
nøglekort key card
nål n pin (brooch); needle

O

objektiv lens (camera)
og and
også also; too
omkring around (approximately)
omkørsel detour (traffic)
område region
ondt i halsen sore throat
ondt i ørerne earache
op up
opera opera; opera house
operation operation
oplukker bottle opener
opsparingskonto savings account
optaget busy; occupied
optiker optician
opvarme v heat
opvaskemaskine dishwasher
opvaskemiddel detergent
orange orange (color)
ord word
ordbog dictionary
orkester orchestra
oval oval
ovenpå above; upstairs

overfald n attack; mugging
overfart crossing (maritime)
overfor opposite
overførsel transfer (money wire)
overskud n profit
overskæg moustache
overslag n estimate
oversætte translate
overtjener head waiter
ovn stove
oxygenbehandling oxygen treatment

P

pakke package [parcel BE]
papir paper
papirhandel stationery store
papirhåndklæde paper towel
papirslommetørklæde tissue
par pair
paraply umbrella
parfume perfume
park n park
parkering parking
parkeringskælder parking garage
parkeringsplads parking lot [car park BE]
parkeringsskive parking disc
parkometer parking meter
pas passport
pasfoto passport photo

paskontrol passport control
passe *v* fit
patient patient
pc computer
pedicure pedicure
pege *v* point
pen pen
penge money
pengeautomat ATM
penicillin penicillin
pensionat guesthouse
pensioneret retired
pensionist senior citizen
per dag per day
per person per person
per time per hour
per uge per week
perle pearl
perron platform (station)
person person
personale staff
personlig personal
petit petite
pibe pipe
pige girl
pille pill; tablet (medical)
pincet tweezers
pinkode PIN
plads seat
pladsreserveringen reservations
  office

planetarium planetarium
plaster *n* bandage [plaster BE]
plastic plastic
plasticpose plastic bag
plastikfolie plastic wrap
platin platinum
plet stain
plombe filling (tooth)
pløk peg (tent)
politi police
politianmeldelse police report
politistation police station
porcelæn porcelain
portier porter
portion portion
porto postage
post *n* mail [post BE]
postanvisning money order
poste restante general delivery
posthus post office
postkasse mailbox [postbox BE]
postkort postcard
pottemageri pottery
praktiserende læge doctor [general
  practitioner BE]
presse press (iron)
pris price
privat private
procentsats percentage
program program (of events)
proptrækker corkscrew

protese denture
præsentation introduction (social)
præsentere introduce
præventivmiddel contraceptive
prøverum fitting room
pudder powder
pude pillow
pumpe pump
pund pound (British currency, weight)
punktering puncture
pyjamas pajamas
pære light bulb
på on
på landet countryside
pålidelig reliable

R

rabat discount
rabatkort booklet (of tickets)
radio radio
rav amber
reb rope
recept prescription
reception reception
receptionist receptionist
redningsbælte life preserver
redningsbåd life boat
redningsvest life jacket
regnemaskine calculator
regnfrakke raincoat

regning check [bill BE] (restaurant)
regnvejr rain
rejse journey; travel; trip
rejsebureau travel agency
rejsecheck traveler's check [cheque BE]
rejsefører guidebook
rejsefører travel guide
rektangulær rectangular
religion religion
ren clean; pure
rensecreme cleansing cream
renseri dry cleaner
rente interest (finance)
reparation n repair
reparere v fix; mend
reservation reservation
reserveret reserved
rest n rest
restaurant restaurant
ret dish (food item)
retsbygning court house
returbillet round-trip [return BE] ticket
returnere return (come back)
reumatisme rheumatism
ribben rib
ridning horseback riding
rigtigt right (correct)
ring ring (jewelry)
ringeklokke bell (electric)

rive i stykker *v* tear
robåd rowboat
rolig calm
romantisk romantic
roomservice room service
rubin ruby
rullegardin blind (window)
rulletrappe escalator
rumtemperatur room temperature
rund round
runde round (golf)
rundt om around (the corner)
rundtur sightseeing tour
rustfrit stål stainless steel
rute route
ryg back
ryge smoke
rygrad spine
rygsæk backpack
rød red
røntgenfotografere X-ray
røre *v* touch
rådhus town hall

S

safir sapphire
saks scissors
sal hall (room)
saldo balance (finance)
salg *n* sale
samme same

sand sand
sandal sandal
sang song
satin satin
sauna sauna
scooter scooter
se *v* look
seddel bill (bank note)
sejlbåd sailboat
sekund second
sele seat belt
sende send
senere later
seng bed
sent late (time)
separeret separated (relationship)
servere serve (meal)
service på værelset room service
serviet napkin
seværdighed point of interest
shampoo shampoo
side side
siden since
sidst last
sige tell
sightseeing sightseeing
sikker *adj* safe
sikkerhedsnål safety pin
silke silk
skaffe provide
skak chess

skakspil chess set
skarp sharp (pain)
skat tax
ske spoon
skib n ship
skilt notice (sign)
skive n slice
skjorte shirt
sko shoe
skodde shutter (window)
skoforretning shoe store
skole school
Skotland Scotland
skov forest
skovl n shovel
skrald garbage [rubbish BE]
skrive write
skrive recept på prescribe
skruetrækker screwdriver
skrædder tailor
skubbe v push
skulder shoulder
skulle have (must)
skulptur sculpture
sky cloud
skæg beard
skøjte v skate
skøjtebane skating rink
skønhedssalon beauty salon
slags sort (kind)
slagter butcher

slebet glas cut glass
slette v clear
slips tie
slipseklemme tie clip
slot palace
sluge swallow
slutning end
smal narrow
smaragd emerald
smerte ache; pain
smerter i brystet chest pain
smerter i ryggen backache
smertestillende middel analgesic; painkiller
sminke n make-up
smitsom contagious
smuk beautiful
snackbar snack bar
snart soon
snevejr snow
snitsår n cut (wound)
snor string
snorkeludstyr snorkeling equipment
sokke sock
sol sun
solbriller sunglasses
solcreme sun-tan lotion
solforbrænding sunburn
solid sturdy
solstik sunstroke

sort black
souvenir souvenir
souvenirbutik souvenir shop
sove v sleep
sovepille sleeping pill
sovepose sleeping bag
sovevogn sleeping car
spa spa
spand bucket; pail
spatel spatula
specialist specialist
specialitet speciality
spejl mirror
spil game
spillehal arcade
spillekort playing card
spise eat
spiseolie oil
spisesalen dining room
spisevogn dining car
spor track (train)
sport sport
sportsforretning sporting goods store
sporvogn tram
springvand fountain
sprog language
spænding voltage
spørgsmål n question
stadium stadium
stave v spell

stearinlys candle
sted n place
stegepande frying pan
stel frame (glasses)
sterlingsølv sterling silver
sti path
stige af get off
stik plug (electric)
stik n sting
stikkontakt electrical outlet
stikpille suppository
stille quiet
stilling occupation
stjerne star
stjæle steal
stof cloth; fabric; material
stol chair
stoppet blocked
stor big; large
stor størrelse plus-size
storartet great (excellent)
Storbritannien Great Britain
stormagasin department store
strand beach
strikvarer knitwear
strygejern iron (clothing)
strøm current (ocean)
strømpe stockings
strømpebukser panty hose
studere study
studerende student

studsning trim
stuepige maid
stykke piece; play (theater)
stærk strong
stævnemøde date (appointment)
støjende noisy
størrelse size
støvle boot
støvsuger vacuum cleaner
stå op get up
sulten hungry
supermarked supermarket
sut pacifier [dummy BE] (baby's)
sutteflaske baby bottle
svamp sponge
svar answer
svimmel dizzy
svimmingpool pool
svuppert plunger
svær difficult
svømme *v* swim
svømmebassin pool
svømning swimming
sweater sweater
sweatshirt sweatshirt
sy sew
syd south
syg ill [BE]
sygdom disease; illness
sygeforsikring health insurance
sygeplejerske nurse

symbol symbol
syn eyesight
synagoge synagogue
synge sing
synshæmmet visually impaired
syntetisk synthetic
system system
sæbe soap
sæde ved midtergangen aisle seat
sælge sell
særlig special
sæson season
sætning sentence
sætte put
sætte sig sit down
sø lake
sød sweet
sølv silver
sølvtøj silverware
så then
sår wound

T

tab loss
tage take
tage imod *v* accept
tage med bring; to go
  [take away BE]
tage mål af measure
tage tøjet af undress
taget taken (occupied)

tak thank you
takke thank
tale *v* speak
tallerken plate
tampon tampon
tand tooth
tandbørste toothbrush
tandlæge dentist
tandpasta toothpaste
tandpine toothache
tarm bowel
taske case (camera)
taske bag (purse)
taxa taxi
taxaholdeplads taxi stand [rank BE]
teater theater
tegnebog wallet
telefon *n* telephone
telefonbog telephone directory
telefonboks telephone booth
telefonist operator
telefonkort phone card
telefonnummer telephone number
telt tent
teltpløk tent peg
teltstang tent pole
teltunderlag groundsheet
tempel temple
temperatur temperature
tennisbane tennis court
tenniskamp tennis match

tennisketsjer tennis racket
terminal terminal
termometer thermometer
terrasse terrace
teske teaspoon
tid *n* time
tidligt early
til to
til lykke congratulations
til tiden on time
til venstre left
tilbehør accessory
tillæg *n* supplement
time hour (time)
tinlegering pewter
tjekke ud *v* check out
tjener waiter
tobak tobacco
tobakshandler tobacconist
tog train
togkort subway [underground BE] map
toilet restroom [toilet BE]
toiletartikel toiletry
toiletpapir toilet paper
told customs; duty
toldangivelsesformular customs declaration form
toldfri butik duty-free shop
toldfri varer duty-free goods
tolk interpreter

tom empty
tommelfinger thumb
torden thunder
tordenvejr thunderstorm
trafiklys traffic light
transportabel portable
trappe stairs
travlt hurry
trist gloomy
tro think (believe)
tryk pressure
træ tree
trække *v* pull
trække vejret breathe
trækul charcoal
træt tired
tråd thread
trådløs wireless
T-shirt T-shirt
tube tube
tung heavy
tunge tongue
tur tour
turistkontor tourist office
tynd thin
tyv thief
tyveri robbery
tyveri theft
tæppe blanket
tøj clothing
tøjbutik clothing store

tør dry
tørklæde scarf
tørstig thirsty
tå toe
tåge fog
tårn tower

U

uden without
udenfor outside
udenlandsk foreign
udenrigsfly international flight
udflugt excursion
udfylde fill in (form)
udgang *n* exit
udgift expense
udkigspost *n* overlook
udlejning rental
udlejningsbil rental car
udsalg sale (bargains)
udsigt view (panorama)
udskrive *v* print (document)
udslet rash
udsolgt out of stock; sold out
udspecificeret regning itemized bill
udstilling exhibition
udstillingsmontre display case
udstyr appliance; equipment
udtale pronunciation
udtryk expression

uge week
uld wool
ulykke accident
under under
underbukser underpants
underkop saucer
underlig strange
underrette notify
underskrift signature
underskrive sign
undersøgelse check-up (medical)
undertrøje undershirt
undervisning lesson
undskylde v excuse
ung young
universitet university
ur clock; watch
USA United States
uskyldig innocent

V

vaccinere vaccinate
valuta currency
vand water
vandfald waterfall
vandhane faucet
vandrehjem youth hostel
vandski waterski
vandtæt waterproof
vare article (merchandise)
varm hot; warm (temperature)

varme heat [heating BE]
vaske i hånden hand washable
vaske v wash
vaskemaskine washing machine
vaskeri laundry service
vaskerum laundry facilities
vaskesuger plunger
vasketøj laundry
ved at
ved siden af next to
vedhæng pendant
vegetar vegetarian
vej road; way
vejangivelse direction
vejkort road map
vejkryds crossroads; intersection
vejr weather
vejrudsigt weather forecast
vejskilt road sign
vekselkontor currency exchange office
vekselkurs exchange rate
veksle v exchange (money)
ven friend
vending phrase
vene vein
vente v expect; wait
venteværelse waiting room
ventilator fan
vest west
v-hals v-neck

vi we
vide know
videokamera video camera
vigtig important
vil gerne like
ville have want
vind wind
vindue window
vinduessæde window seat
vinhandel liquor store [off-licence BE]
vinliste wine list
violet purple
virke *v* work
virkelig hyggelig wonderful
virker ikke out of order
vis certain
vise vej til *v* direct (someone)
visitkort business card
viskelæder eraser
voldtægt *n* rape
volleyballkamp volleyball game
væddeløb race
væddeløbsbane race track
væk away
vække wake
vækkeur alarm clock
vælg choice
vær venlig please
værdi value
være be

værelse room (hotel)
værelsesbestillig hotel reservation
værelsesnummer room number
værktøj tool
værre worse
væske fluid
vådservietter baby wipes

W

Wales Wales
weekend weekend
windsurfer windsurfer

Z

zoologisk have zoo

Æ

ædelsten gem
ægte genuine; real
ændre *v* alter
ærme sleeve
æske box

Ø

øje eye
øjeblik moment
øjendråber eye drops
øjenskygge eye shadow
økonomiklasse economy class
øm sore (painful)
ønske *v* wish
øre ear